I0824884

WHAT STAYS and WHAT GOES

ORGANIZE WITH INTENTION and CREATE SPACE FOR GRACE

FAITH ROBERSON

SCRIBNER

New York Amsterdam/Antwerp London
Toronto Sydney/Melbourne New Delhi

Scribner
An Imprint of Simon & Schuster, LLC
1230 Avenue of the Americas
New York, NY 10020

First Scribner hardcover edition April 2026

Interior design by Laura Levatino

Manufactured in the United States of America

10 9 8 7 6 5 4 3 2 1

Library of Congress Control Number has been applied for.

ISBN 978-1-6680-1174-4
ISBN 978-1-6680-1175-1 (ebook)

For Azeen

CONTENTS

Part Three: Social Work

WHAT STAYS
and
WHAT GOES

INTRODUCTION

IN THIS BOOK, we will explore three principles of organization: *awareness, boundaries*, and *adjustments*. These are more than strategies for organizing our homes. They are the framework of this narrative.

PART ONE: SOUL WORK is about *awareness*: examining our relationship to ourselves and our belongings. Awareness isn't about springing into action, or fixing a problem. It's about exploring the patterns that shape us and the spaces we inhabit. It's about gathering insight and giving ourselves time to assess and understand what we've lived through and learned. Awareness sheds light on where we can evolve.

If we want change, we must first become aware of ourselves and the world around us. Like a tree sheds its leaves in autumn, we must recognize what no longer serves us and release it. The journey to awareness has no end; as long as we're living, we'll continue to discover newness. Awareness is a cycle—it is something we must choose again and again.

In sharing my story, and the stories of others, I aim to show how deeply connected we are by universal themes. No matter our race, class, gender, or age, we often wrestle with similar issues in our homes. The details may differ, the cost of our possessions may vary, yet at the core the lesson is the same: *how to let go in order to grow.*

PART TWO: HOME WORK examines *boundaries* and the practice of organizing our surroundings and ourselves—our minds, ethics, relationships to others. Boundaries aren't rigid walls that confine or exclude us. They're lines that can move in response to what's needed. These lines guide, restore, and reveal the creativity and variety of life. Boundaries frame what we see and how we engage with the world.

Organizing allows us to determine what takes precedence in our lives. On the surface, we may use boundaries to curtail clutter. However, boundaries are more than that. They make way for balance. That is what home work is: the intimate process of balancing our surroundings to support who we are and what we need. It's creative, soulful, and profoundly personal work. Boundaries make space for change.

PART THREE: SOCIAL WORK is about *adjustments*. We are called to be in a community with one another and to work toward a collaborative greater good. By identifying the narratives that keep us disconnected from and uninterested in uplifting one another, we examine how our personal choices affect our society and how our culture affects us.

If awareness sheds light on our lives and boundaries give those lives shape, then adjustments are how we settle into those shapes. Adjustments recalibrate the systems we've built, allowing us to stay in tempo with life and know when it's time to change.

Homemaking is a powerful practice. When it transforms us personally, others feel it too. In several chapters, I offer reflective questions that hold space for us to examine the larger systems and social constructs that influence our decisions and our sense of self. Yet, the choices we make—what stays and what goes, how we consume, or what we value—impact our lives beyond the domestic sphere. At every stage, we will practice feeling compassion, accepting change, making difficult decisions, releasing what no longer works, and choosing to move forward. As we cultivate these skill sets, we will practice how to care for our homes and learn how to live in harmony with others.

PART ONE
SOUL WORK

CHAPTER 1

AN ACT OF FAITH

As a child, seeing the word *faith* written on church merchandise or hearing it ring through pastors' sermons on Sundays somehow made me feel it was about me. In my self-centered youth (steeped in religion, growing up poor), carrying this name sometimes felt like a burden. My name could trigger emotional responses in strangers, who would tell me about their lives. How they had just prayed to God for faith, whether the night before, that morning, or on the car ride to wherever they found me.

These run-ins would happen in the parking lot at Kmart, in line at Goodwill, or while I was sitting in the waiting room of the doctor's office. People took meeting me as the sign for which they had prayed. I would try to release my hand from my mother's and make my escape as people shared their woes with us. Mama would squeeze me tightly while swapping war stories and thanking God, before saying goodbye. "Let God use you," she lovingly advised me on our way home. She knew my name provided others with a sense of hope.

In time, I would learn to listen patiently as people shared things I had not asked to hear about. I would come to appreciate the meaning of my name as I got older. In the course of my life, I have dealt with setbacks and conflicts that required me to embrace faith. I had to believe in my ability to take the pieces of my life to build something greater, and know that even if I failed in my endeavors, I would learn from my mistakes and find the courage to carry on.

My ideas about home, like everyone else's, are shaped by the places I've lived and the people I've lived with. These foundational experiences led me to become a professional organizer and to start my company, Organize With Faith. My philosophy is that faith is a critical ingredient for organizing your life. Faith is the difference between where we are today and where we want to be. To make a home that is uniquely ours, we must be intentional about the spaces we create. Operating with faith gives us the confidence that we are capable of making these spaces for ourselves. Faith is not the big finale: It's applied every step of the way.

* * *

WHEN I WAS GROWING UP, my mama kept an impeccable home—or dare I say, we kept an impeccable home. My brother, sister, and I shared the chores. My mama never stressed us about keeping our rooms clean, but the communal spaces were always tidy. "Y'all have it easy," she laughed whenever we complained about our domestic responsibilities. "Your aunt, uncles, and I soldiered through your granny's house on assignment every single day. We stripped beds, washed and hung clothes to dry, ironed linens, and waxed the floors." She emphasized the word *waxed*, neatly dividing our upbringing from her own.

Whereas we simply mopped, she and her siblings mopped and then waxed. Whereas we wiped down the kitchen cabinets, they removed all the dishes, disinfected the shelves, and then wiped down the cabinets. We loaded the dishwasher, but they towel-dried and put the dishes away every night. Then came the yard work—raking leaves, pulling weeds, feeding livestock. With her hand on her hip, my mama liked to brag about her childhood labor, her eyes gleaming with pride.

One afternoon, my aunt Carla, Mama's sister, came over to our house but no one was home. Carla let herself in with the spare key and made a sandwich in the kitchen. After eating her sandwich, my aunt cleaned her dishes, returned them to the cabinet, wiped down the counter, then locked the door after she left.

A few hours later, my mother called my aunt and whispered suspiciously, "Carla, I think someone has been in my house."

"What would make you think that?" Aunt Carla asked.

"There was a crumb on the counter!" Mama replied. Amazed at my mother's awareness, Aunt Carla confessed she had been the intruder who must have left a crumb on the counter. They roared with laughter. My mother explained that she had cleaned the kitchen before going out that morning, paying particular attention to a stain on that countertop. What I love most about this story is not her attention to detail but rather her connection to the space.

There was not a corner in our home that Mama did not know. She worked hard to afford what we had, so we handled every object with care. According to her, a home was not about what you had, or how much it cost, but how you cared for your belongings. Caring for your space reaffirms the work you do to deserve it.

Our house was always organized and neat, without the expense of storage containers. My mama did not style our closets with baskets and boxes, yet they still looked good. To pull a basket off a shelf to grab a container holding a box of Band-Aids would have driven her crazy. Those hurdles would not constitute an organized house. They would just be a nuisance.

I once asked her what makes a house feel like a home. She told me the trick: You must engage all five senses. Think about what you hear or what others hear when they first walk through the door. Is music playing or are wind chimes tinkling in the background? What you *hear* sets the tone of your home. Your nose lets you know how a space is being cared for. When you *smell* the coffee brewing in the morning or food cooking, those are scents of *presence*. Neglected spaces have . . . less pleasant smells.

What you *see* is either an invitation to relax and stay awhile or something that makes you want to leave. A few folded blankets or quilts near the sofa invite you to kick up your feet. The soft light of candles adds an alluring element of warmth that makes your guests want to linger. If the entryways are cluttered and the corner chair is piled high with laundry, the visual evidence of these unfinished chores interrupts the serenity of the space.

Taste is about nourishing your body and mind. An offering to a guest (or yourself) can be simple—like a cup of tea, a piece of chocolate, or a bowl of chili on colder days. My mother always kept the pantry well stocked, preferably with dried beans, brown rice, flour, and sugar. That way, even if the money ran low, you knew you could still eat.

For the last sense, remember this: What you feel triggers how you feel. The sense of *touch* is central to feeling secure. The coziness of a plush chair or the softness of your linens promotes comfort and relaxation. What we feel at home extends beyond the décor. Beyond physical touch lies the emotional and spiritual energy that occupy a space, shaping our experiences in ways we don't always realize. What is felt within the spaces we inhabit is as much about our beliefs and values as are the pillows we rest our heads on. I learned this from my mama—not through her master class on the five senses but by sharing that space with her, navigating the weight of things that were both within and beyond her control.

* * *

MY GRANNY WAS THE HEART of her home. Summers at her house near California's Lake Nacimiento were quiet and bountiful. There were biscuits rising in the sun on the porch, the fish she and I had caught that morning lying in the sink, a homemade cake on the counter, and an unfinished puzzle on a folding table out back. My grandfather, the town butcher, always came home full-handed. On any given night, there would be a feast of oxtails with mustard, pork ribs, grits, collard greens, and salmon croquettes, followed by smooth malted milkshakes or frothy root beer floats for dessert. My grandparents lived in a modest two-bedroom mobile home. Together, they welcomed whoever would drive the winding road to get there. Guests entered the house through an unlocked door that led directly to my grandmother, who would be reclining in a worn leather chair in a dimly lit room. The house was not bright, but it sparkled nonetheless.

The lessons my mother taught me about chores and home-making were the same ones her mother had taught her: the value in making something out of nothing. My grandmother kept a beautiful home. It wasn't an Instagram-niche beauty. It was real life beauty—underestimated beauty, ubiquitously ordinary salt-of-the-earth beauty. When you stepped into her home, it felt like the entire room stood up to greet you. A snagged thread on her loveseat might rub your back while the throw she had crocheted by hand embraced you. She infused every piece of furniture, every fabric, plate, and pitcher with soul.

There she was, laying hands on the framed photographs that hung in the hallway, blessing the food Pop had brought in, humming hymns out the window, and whispering prayers before bed. She held church every day in her home. Having a clean house that was always prepared for unexpected visitors was critical to her. What inspired us all was her emphasis on hospitality and comfort—elements that create a warm and inviting atmosphere.

I remember once that there were rumors circulating through the town about a woman whose husband had left her. After a few Sundays had passed and she was not at church, my grandmother went over to her house, knocked on her door, and said, "You are coming with me." Granny took the woman back to her house and put her to work cleaning. Over a bucket of soapy water, they grieved together. As they shared stories of heartbreak and regret, they laughed, cried, and tidied up. I always wondered if the purpose of that visit was to get the woman to open up, or if Granny simply wanted her house cleaned. Whatever the reason, the housework had helped. I guess Granny figured that when life knocks you off your feet, you might as well grab a bucket of hot water and get to work. In truth, cleaning your house has the power to change your point of view.

* * *

WHEN I WASN'T at Granny's home of warmth, or my mother's house of perfection, I spent time in a different kind of communal space—one built on discipline, evolution, and structure. For most of my childhood, my father lived in a commune. My parents had divorced before I was born, and so split custody was established. Most weekdays and two weekends a month, I would stay with my mother in rural Paso Robles, California. I spent every other weekend and Wednesday nights with my father at Roanoke, the commune where he lived, in a sleepy beach town twenty miles away. The two-story house was old, cold, and restless, with rustic floors that creaked and a guano tin roof whose dull skylight lured seagulls to crash into it.

The Roanoke building was split into two sections, one floor for women, where I slept, and one for men. The commune thrived on reciprocity—the more you gave, the more you would receive. The church opened every morning at 6 a.m. for roll call and worship. Anyone who missed roll call would be woken by my father, who marched down the halls with a megaphone on full blast: "Roanoke is a working Christian commune—emphasis on work. If you are not working, then you must leave the premises." Roanoke residents contributed to the effort by cooking, gardening, painting, beekeeping, fishing, or doing construction projects. Assignments were issued daily, and Roanoke's mission prevailed throughout: Get to work and work together.

If you had issues with another house member, a rule, or an assignment (and people had plenty), you aired them at the weekly grievance session. The grievance session was a mandatory meeting held on Wednesday evenings, which I enjoyed attending. These meetings aimed to rectify conflict between members, assess complaints, and codify policies and systems. Living and working so closely together meant these weekly check-ins were required. I sat in awe as disputes clouded the room and then were resolved. These meetings etched a mural of intimate interactions between the ever-evolving residents and the unflappability of Roanoke as an institution. Roanoke sought to protect the commune's core values and long-standing principles.

Nothing annoyed the members more than the requisite dorm shuffle, citing that everyone must change dorm rooms every four to six weeks. People did not like moving. I asked my father why they had to do this. "We don't want them to get too comfortable," he said. According to my father, Roanoke was not a place to stay long-term but served as a passageway from one place or state of being to another. Each dorm room was a cocoon, a preparation site before assimilating back into society. Moving caused disorientation, disrupted the habits of everyday life, and sparked changes in thought, lifestyle, and identity. The dorm shuffle was often the thing that pushed residents to pursue a home of their own.

Whether members were open to a transformation or not, change was thrust upon them. I began to see this way of living as an exercise in flexibility. Disrupting what we're used to presents us with an opportunity to create something new. As we rebuild our spaces, we rebuild our lives. Consequently, our perspective changes as we are forced to reimagine our relationships with ourselves, with others, with our space, and with our things.

* * *

I GREW UP IN A "What happens in the house stays in the house" kind of family. Personal challenges, especially while we were in the thick of them, were often swept under the rug. Adults might discuss what God had brought them through—but only after the hardship had passed. More complicated situations weren't always spoken about. Instead, you prayed for the strength to endure. My mother, like many others, was carrying wounds that prayer alone could not heal. As a child, I didn't fully understand what she was battling, but I could feel its presence in our home. Her prayers vacillated between victory and defeat. She, like the women before her, had been taught that healing meant being strong, which hardened her. Over the years, our home became a place of tension, where love existed but seemed buried beneath unspoken truths.

I was an independent, headstrong adolescent. I took after my father in more ways than I imagine my mother would have liked. With my older siblings gone, the spotlight was on me. My mother was a perfectionist, the type of woman who would hover over you while you cut carrots to make sure every slice was the same thickness. My father, on the other hand, was free-range in his parenting style. Where she was strict, he was lenient. Where her temper was short, he was merciful. The older I got, the more I craved his presence. The more I wanted to stay with him, the more she tightened her grip; the harder she held on, the more I resisted. We became locked in a battle that neither of us could win.

The space was not to blame. My mother was always an exceptional homemaker. But the atmosphere was suffocating. While my childhood had seasons of joy, my teenage years were far from happy. The warmth I longed for felt conditional and unpredictable. After one particularly fraught confrontation, I went to school and, in a panic, I called my father from the counselor's office. "I'm not going back there," I told him. I expected him to reassure me, to tell me to hold on, to convince me to return home. He didn't. Maybe he sensed what I already knew: If I stayed, the relationship between my mother and me might break beyond repair.

Roanoke was not a place for someone my age to live full-time. So, I bunked at my aunt's house and once the dust had settled, I moved in with my elementary-school librarian, Mrs. Erwin, who had more room. We had stayed in contact after I graduated elementary school. I volunteered at the library after hours throughout the seventh and eighth grade. After organizing and tidying up the bookshelves, she would drive me home in her white Sebring convertible. As we passed by, we'd wave to my friends walking home. I often referred to her as my Fairy Godmother.

The Erwins lived with their son in a ranch-style house at the top of a hill. If I hitched a ride home with a friend from choir rehearsal, I'd usually be dropped off at the bottom. The hill was so steep and the road so narrow that most people were wary of driving all the way up. Left in the dust, I took the shortcut through sticky weeds and sandy dirt, stomping through wild grass that was dried out from seasons without rain. Occasionally, I would see Mrs. Erwin, sitting on the deck and smoking a cigarette, as I waved on my way up.

The day I moved in with the Erwins, my father delivered my belongings from my mother's house. His Chevy pickup was packed with trash bags of clothes and stuffed animals, along with boxes filled with journals and textbooks. When he arrived, the Erwins showed him to my room. We made our way through the sunken living room and the kitchen, with its glass shelves suspended by metal rods (a few months later, the shaking from an earthquake would cause those shelves to swing wildly and send all the wine-glasses crashing down).

For weeks, I had been living without my possessions, but once they arrived, I wanted to give them all back. My mother had packed up every single thing I owned. At the time, I took this as a sign she wanted me gone as much as I wanted to leave. Later, much later, I wondered if that was her attempt to prepare me with whatever I might need to move forward.

My things were now mine to manage; the baggage was mine to carry. I would be the one to decide what, if anything, I wanted to hold on to. As I unpacked, I thought of the Roanoke dorm shuffle, with its people disoriented, trying to make their things fit in a new space. I attempted the same, arranging everything in my new room in a still unfamiliar house.

The Erwins were the middle ground between the two conflicting lifestyles of my parents: They offered support without rigidity, freedom without neglect. Even so, I felt unmoored. I had broken the family rule—what happens in the house, stays in the house. Many relatives disapproved of my living with the Erwins. My siblings could not understand why I wouldn't go home. This house may have had the peace I was seeking, but it wasn't home. It never could offer the love of my mother—her hugs, laughter, and wisdom. I'd think about this every time I reached into one of those boxes, pulling out a sweater she'd neatly folded or a journal she had carefully packed. Even in our distance, she was present.

On Saturdays, I would help Mrs. Erwin do the laundry. We would sort her husband's and son's dirty clothes into piles. Before loading the washer, we would empty all the pants pockets. "If you find any money, you get to keep it," she told me.

"What do you mean?" I asked.

"We're doing their laundry. If they don't care enough to empty their pockets first, whatever we find, we keep. If they don't like it, they can do their own laundry." I nodded back and smiled. I had never been in a home where people left money in their pockets. Her son, Paul, worked at a restaurant, and he often had scrunched-up tens and twenties from tips deep in his jeans. The day I found a hundred-dollar bill I started jumping up and down with my arms raised, hollering, "Bingo!"

Mrs. Erwin gave me a high five and said, "It's all yours." After that day, we never found any money in his pockets.

Paul Erwin was in his early twenties, and he always kept his bedroom door open. His room was a disaster. Unlike Paul, I kept my door closed. My bedroom was my safe haven, a space to process the situation I was in. One day I came home from school and shut the door to my room. I was on a mission. I pulled everything out of every drawer and closet. The items scattered on the floor flooded my senses with memories. Memories of Christmases or birthdays when she'd given me stuffed animals, or picture frames we picked out at garage sales. Among those pleasant memories, though, were objects that evoked deeply unhappy feelings. My journals were filled with stories of anguish and rage. My handwriting was big, and the words crossed the lines on the paper because I had been so upset when I wrote them.

I flipped through the pages of those journals, searching for something good. I had recorded our arguments in detail, but for what reason? I began to break the bindings and I used scissors to snip the string that held the pages together. With each snip I imagined gaining freedom from her judgment. As I began tearing the pages, I imagined tearing myself away from the hate that was written on each line. Almost all those pages went into the trash. But I used that moment to forgive myself and my mother for the mess we made, the bond we broke, and the pain we caused each other. I then stuffed a few pages into the slender neck of a glass bottle. I kept that bottle on my desk as a reminder of what I had been through. The bottle also served as a talisman of the love that still existed between us, even when it was buried beneath resentment.

Discarding my old journals was the beginning of a lifelong decluttering journey. I didn't do it to make my space look better. I did it to help me make peace with my past. Letting go was difficult, but by seeing my journals as a physical representation of my anger, I was able to begin processing my feelings. This gesture of mindfully letting go of possessions—particularly those charged with painful memories—cleared a path to move forward. Although I didn't know it at the time, that was the start of the Soul Work I do now with my clients. Together we explore the internal and emotional aspects of decluttering. The introspection of Soul Work allows people to release the hold their belongings may have on them.

* * *

BY LETTING GO, I opened up space in my life for a new way of living, yet I was unsure of what to do next. Despite the generosity of my new guardians, I struggled emotionally. Once a week I went to therapy, where I shared feelings of hopelessness. I was in limbo—I didn't totally fit in at the Erwins', and the fracture between me and my mother had left me on the outs with my family. There was nothing the Erwins could do that would make me happy. After months of suicidal ideations, I checked myself into a psychiatric facility. I was assigned an all-white room with a single bed. I plopped myself down on the thin mattress. I could feel the springs pressing against my back as I stared up at the ceiling. I slept the days away to the sound of rain. On the third day, my grandmother arrived. She entered my room soaking wet, holding a broken umbrella.

"Faith, it's time you come home. You don't have to go back to your mother's house, but you can't stay here."

"Where will I go?" I asked.

"You'll live with me," she said.

"Where will I sleep?" I cried, picturing the one-bedroom apartment to which my grandmother had downsized when my grandfather moved into assisted living, several hours away.

"You'll sleep with me," she said. A few days later I moved in.

I had pared down significantly while living at the Erwins', which seemed serendipitous now that I was in an apartment with only one closet. I began unpacking my clothes, sandwiching them between Granny's church dresses. I placed my shoes under the bed. But Granny and I were a match made in heaven. She was unapologetic about her life. She would open up to me about her mistakes and imperfections in hopes that I would learn from her experience. This made me able to confide in her in a way I couldn't with other adults in my life.

After dinner each night I would make us malted milkshakes while Granny raised the head of the bed so we could watch Lifetime movies. Then we'd talk until we fell asleep. The topics were endless—her childhood in Arkansas, boys, sex, and her becoming a mother at fifteen. Most nights, we held hands while she listed her regrets and cried about how much she missed Pop. Or, we would laugh and gossip about church members, family, and her neighbors. I shared with her my dreams of leaving our small town and moving to New York City. "Have you ever been there?" I asked one night, my belly full of fried chicken and black-eyed peas.

"I have," she smiled. While Granny told me about her adventures in Washington, DC, and Manhattan, her face lit up. I realized then she was more than just my grandmother—she was a woman with her own hopes and dreams.

As I settled into living in her apartment, relishing her attention and care, my depression began to fade. On weekends, while she visited Pop in the assisted-living facility, I cooked and cleaned. After a few months, I decided to rearrange the furniture in the living room. I pushed the couch to the adjacent wall and I moved a side table from our bedroom beside it. I pulled out a rug from under the bed, vacuuming the paisley print before setting it under the coffee table. After doing laundry, I moved the slips and girdles Granny no longer wore to the top shelf of the closet, so I could get myself one more dresser drawer. When she returned home, I gave her a tour. She looked around, then took my hand.

"Faith, I have something to tell you," she said.

"You don't like it?" I asked. We never discussed my moving the furniture or her things, but I didn't think she would mind.

"Faith, I have to move to be closer to Pop." My heart sank. Two days later, my father was back with his Chevy pickup to haul my things to my aunt's house, where I stayed for the remainder of my high school days.

Moving away from Granny took a piece of my heart. She'd done for me what no one else could do—she helped me get back on track, imagining a life beyond our town. In retrospect, I can see the through lines: how the culture of a home is defined by its members. Carving out one's own space is key to feeling a sense of belonging, even if it's a little space, for a little while.

* * *

I LEARNED EARLY that life is a series of moves—some we choose, and some are chosen for us. Despite difficulties, we can still love ourselves. We can nurture, listen to, and meet our emotional needs. As someone who has been on a homemaking quest for most of my life, I believe home is not a place but an action. Home is what we carry with us, what we build for ourselves, and the history we grapple with in the privacy of our spaces. Home is a relationship we tend, a space we nurture within ourselves and with one another. Home is *grace*.

REFLECTIVE QUESTIONS

When you think of home, ask yourself:

- Do I have faith in my capacity to create the home I desire?
- What have I learned from my past?
- How do I apply those teachings to how I choose to live today?
- How do I create a space that feels more like home?
- What does home mean to me?
- In what ways can I nurture the parts of myself that do not feel at home?

CHAPTER 2

THE SPACE BETWEEN US

I MOVED FROM CALIFORNIA to New York City when I was nineteen, just like I'd dreamed. For a while, I hopped around Manhattan, sleeping on friends' couches. My grandmother called often, mostly trying to convince me to return to Paso Robles to find a husband. "I feel like there is something for me here, and I am not going to leave until I find it," I told her.

New York, like the Roanoke commune, has an air of fellowship. Expats and locals alike inhabit a city where you reap what you sow. Blocks are stacked with people living in high-rises, in brownstones, and in public housing developments, melding together through a collective experience: Get to work and work together. I worked a series of odd jobs until I eventually began waitressing.

The farm-to-table café where I worked served breakfast, brunch, and lunch to tourists and joggers who came a block away from Central Park. The delicious food was prepared minimally. As I served vegetables drizzled with olive oil and garnished with fresh herbs and wedged lemons, I began making meals at home in the same way.

When I finally found an apartment with my friend Sarah, it felt like a miracle. It was a two-bedroom in Washington Heights, in the northern part of Manhattan. The back bedroom was too small for either of us, so we agreed to convert the space into a walk-in closet. On my father's first trip to New York City, he bought me an accordion door as a house-warming gift. He mounted it at the entrance to the living room, and that became my bedroom. I threw floor cushions at the foot of my bed, around a coffee table I had found on the street. I arranged the kitchen cabinets the way my mother would, lining up bags of beans, rice, flour, and sugar. Every Saturday, I deep-cleaned the apartment while listening to gospel music. When I scoured the oven or removed the dishes to wipe the interiors of the cabinets, I'd hear her voice in my head, *Take care of what you have.* This apartment was the beginning of my learning how to create a place of my own. Yet I housekept and homemade like my mother did.

I started hosting lavish dinner parties for my friends. During the holidays, I packed the apartment with people. Some would fly in from Honolulu or Atlanta to sit at my table, a Pottery Barn upgrade. I borrowed silver cutlery from my neighbor. After the main course, friends of friends would drop by for dessert and drinks. Later into the night, the keyboard would come out and tipsy guests would harmonize until the break of dawn. There were no noise complaints in the Heights. People were always lingering on the corners, while music blared from parked cars. These were familiar and somewhat comforting sounds amid the chaos of fireworks, sirens, and nonstop block parties.

Soon, friends began gifting me with plates, wineglasses, food processors, and cast-iron skillets, as if for a wedding registry. Those dinner parties played a monumental role in cultivating my sense of family and of belonging in New York. Hosting an intimate dinner party offers the perfect combination of labor and reward. I found tending to the details—the menu, playlist, and seating placement—was well worth the stress when I looked around later and saw everyone having a good time.

While opening my home to others brought me immense joy, it also demanded balance. I began to wonder if by being so focused on hosting, I was losing sight of my own needs.

* * *

MY MOTHER AND I had been talking more frequently. We were careful with each other not to press too hard lest we open old wounds. Perhaps because we both wanted to believe we were, further along in our healing process than we were, I tried to stay with her on a visit to California. Our disagreements started with something small—a comment about my hair, or the way I replied to a question. Then it spiraled into something bigger, something that neither of us could let go of. The trouble was that we could never agree on the turn of events—why I left and why she never called me. So, I packed up and stayed with my cousin, sleeping on the couch. While I lay there, I thought of the space between my mother and me, and the past we needed to rewrite. Healing would not be easy for either of us. Still, hope was there.

Our relationship would began to shift when I learned how to mother myself, and be a friend to her. The more I nurtured me, the more I could show up for her. Eventually, we started mending our relationship, not through grand gestures but through consistently being there for each other. It happened slowly. A conversation in which we didn't fight. A phone call that lasted longer than expected. A visit when I didn't leave early. Our communications felt easier. We still had our moments, but they were less frequent.

I started looking forward to seeing her. To hearing her voice and listening to her stories. To going with her to the flea market and watching her face light up when we found something special. "This would look great on your dining table," she said one day, tapping a Blue Willow gravy boat. I nodded, then asked, "What do you think of these?," holding up a set of brass napkin rings. For the first time in a long time, I wanted her opinion. For the first time in a long time, she gave it gently.

* * *

I MET KEITH on my way home from work one summer night. I watched as he carried a heavy upright bass up two flights of subway stairs. He weaved through a sea of people who rushed to cross the street before the light changed. We both missed the light and were paused at the corner when he smiled and introduced himself. That night, he invited me to the Village Vanguard, a famous club, to listen to jazz. The next day, I went to his apartment for a jam session.

I was surprised by how spacious his home was. The open floor plan of the apartment had a large kitchen and living room, with exposed brick walls. There were three bedrooms and polished wood floors that looked like bars of milk chocolate. Keith had two roommates, both of whom were musicians. They all shared the chores and kept the apartment tidy. The furniture was minimal, leaving space for bands to spontaneously gather in the living room. New sets of people toting drums, saxophones, trumpets, and keyboards would all arrive to play as I sat on the couch listening for hours.

Over dinner, Keith confessed that the night before we met, he had lost hope in his dream of making it as a musician in New York City, and he'd prayed for faith. He felt like we were destined to be together. When one of the roommates announced he was moving out, I subleased my Washington Heights apartment to friends, packed up my things, and moved in with Keith. We had known each other for only three months. Keith and I continued to share the apartment with a third roommate, a touring musician who was rarely home. It was an ideal arrangement since we could not afford the apartment on our own.

We hosted fabulous dinner parties. Keith would play his bass or keyboard and my friends would sing along. Our merriment led to a swift marriage proposal.

I grew up in a deeply religious Southern Baptist community, where a young woman living with her boyfriend was considered a sin. In short, I was better off getting married and divorced than living with a man. I was taught that a woman's purpose in life is to find a husband and my value would be determined by how well I could be of service to him. I was told I would not be blessed if I were not married. I'd watched from afar as this marriage pressure forced my cousins into a wedding frenzy. One after the next, they were walking down the aisle to avoid judgment or guilt.

After we announced our engagement, the women in my family outlined my wifely duties, which mostly revolved around holding my tongue and doing the housekeeping. When Keith's mother came to visit, we picked out colors to paint the living room and bathroom. She showered us with gifts, like new bedding (that she picked out), coffee cups with our initials on them, and matching sets of pajamas. While I was at work, they chose the paint color for our bedroom to match our new comforter, which was the color of . . . phlegm.

Before I came along, the household chores had been divided equally among Keith and his two roommates. I could have—and should have—added myself to the chore list. Instead, I took over the majority of the cooking and cleaning. While my fiancé focused on his music, I buzzed around the house, fluffing pillows and folding laundry.

During this chapter of my life, I thought domesticity was my only passion. Imagine my surprise when I began feeling trapped by the life I'd created. My wedding date was getting closer and I was starting to resent the planning on top of doing all the chores. I would ask Keith to help around the house, but he was busy and would soon forget. Further, my mood was often a point of contention between us. He'd say that the way I asked for help was mean. Although I wasn't yelling, the tone of my voice was "bossy." What had started out as fun—kind of like playing house—quickly soured. I called my mother late one night to ask her advice.

"Faith, I didn't want to marry your daddy," she confessed.

"Mama, you married him twice!" I reminded her. My parents have known each other since childhood. According to my father, my mother promised that the second time around, she would be the perfect housewife. (Perfect, in his view, meant submissive.) She tried, dutifully letting him lead as the man of the house. Despite her sincere efforts, Mama always knew best. Within a few months of their marriage, she'd started sharing her opinions, much to my father's dismay.

She continued. "I did, and I shouldn't have. I love your daddy, but we were better as friends. Granny wanted me to get married, and the next thing I knew, I had the dress, the venue, and the whole town was coming. I had my doubts and I asked my best friend if I was making a mistake, but she said I was having jitters. All I needed was one person to tell me, 'I know you bought the dress and sent out the invitations, but you do not have to do it.' So baby, I'm telling you what I wish someone would have told me: You do not have to get married."

"It seems a little late to cancel," I fretted.

"You know when it's too late? After you say, 'I do.'"

The next day, Keith and I called off the wedding. A few weeks later, we ushered guests who couldn't cancel their flights on an outing to the Bronx Zoo. I did not want to be his wife—or anyone's wife then. When he proposed to me, the women in my life were glad I had "found my man." However, I had never asked myself if *I* wanted to marry *him*. After everyone left town to return home, I moved back to my apartment. I had not stepped foot in there for nearly two years. I walked through each room, inspecting the damage and imagining the possibilities. The walls were grimy, the wooden floors were stained, and the furniture I'd left behind was either broken or no longer wanted. Over the next few months, I worked on clearing and cleaning my apartment.

I reflected on how my granny devoted her days to housekeeping and homemaking—I never saw Pop clean anything. When I moved in with Keith, I had simply repeated that pattern. As a woman, the only way I knew how to take my place in a home was to overextend myself. Growing up with role models whose doors were always open to guests and whose houses were impeccable left me with big shoes to fill. I overcompensated and that came at a cost.

This season of my life taught me that homemaking is not always about creating space for others—for our friends, our partners, and our children to gather and be well. Homemaking is about carving out space for ourselves.

The way I had been homemaking was not for me. It was for the idea of who I believed I was supposed to be. Everything I did at home was for others. While I enjoyed being hospitable, I no longer wanted to suffer for it. After moving back into my apartment, I concluded that my space should first serve me. From then onward, every home I made would have to be for my benefit: It would have to be a place where I could rest, hear my thoughts, and nourish my body, heart, and soul. My home would not be a place for me to perform for others. It would be a place where I could be my authentic self.

In many ways, leaving Keith marked my departure from the homemaker role to which I once felt bound. Our relationship revealed the cost of giving without receiving—of building a life based on others' expectations before considering myself. It also taught me what I needed. Ironically, it was my mother's guidance that encouraged my independence. Perhaps that was what she and I had been seeking—not space from each other but space *for* each other. A place where we could stand as individuals and still be seen.

In reclaiming my home, I was also reclaiming my relationship with my mother. The distance that once separated us was transformed into room where we would heal and choose each other again.

Back in my old apartment, I decided not to get a roommate and I returned the place to the original floor plan. I moved my bed to the primary bedroom and restored a proper living room. I turned the makeshift walk-in closet into my office. The first dinner party I held was just for me. I picked up flowers from the bodega, lit candles, and set the table for one. I poured gravy over mashed potatoes from the Blue Willow gravy boat I hadn't used since Christmas. As I ate, I called my mother to celebrate the home I had finally made my own.

REFLECTIVE QUESTIONS

As you think about how your relationship to others shapes your relationship to your home, ask yourself:

- What domestic duties make you feel overextended?
- What external pressures contribute to that feeling?
- If those pressures did not exist, how would you engage differently with housekeeping or homemaking?
- In what ways do you feel taken advantage of at home? What power have you given away?
- What steps can you take to bring yourself closer to achieving balance?

CHAPTER 3
WHAT STAYS AND WHAT GOES

ALAINA WAS A REGULAR at the restaurant. On Saturday mornings, her family rushed through breakfast before heading out to Long Island for the weekend. During the week, she dined alone, tipping generously to make up for the hours she lingered at her table. Over four years of serving Alaina, we became friends. She was instinctual, witty, polished, and successful. She mentored my entrepreneurial ideas, and I sympathized with her reluctance about housekeeping and her self-professed inability to maintain an organized home.

One morning, she mentioned that her husband was on a business trip and asked if I could cook for her sons while he was gone. Alaina had two full-time nannies, a housekeeper twice a week, and now me. With so much support, I found it hard to believe her house was the mess she described.

When I arrived, I paused in the doorway. The afternoon nanny quietly greeted me. "Where I am from, we don't own so much stuff," she said. I nodded, biting my tongue as I took in the contrast between who I had perceived Alaina to be and the clutter before me. Every room sat in limbo, as if they were either packing boxes to move out or in the process of unpacking to stay. I could see why Alaina barely spent any time at home. Still, I couldn't picture her living like this—yanking clothes from heaps on the floor, rummaging through boxes for documents, and stuffing unopened mail into bins overflowing with papers.

When Alaina arrived, she explained that she never liked this apartment. The lease was supposed to be temporary, but time stretched on. Refusing to unpack was her way of protesting the space. Beyond that, she said her husband, Robert, wasn't any help. They both worked full-time, yet the responsibility for managing the home fell entirely on her. "Robert acts like it's my job to put this apartment together—a place [where] I don't even want to live."

I spent the week cooking for Alaina's family. When Robert returned, the couple offered me a regular gig preparing meals. Over time, I found myself staying an extra hour or two to tidy up their kitchen—decluttering the fridge, reorganizing the pantry. Being in their space reignited my passion for domesticity. I wanted to extend my services beyond cooking and tackle the disorganization swallowing their home. One evening, as I packed their meals into Tupperware containers, I pitched the idea to Alaina. At the time, I didn't know professional organizing was a business. I only knew they needed help beyond what a housekeeper could provide.

She was intrigued. We walked through the apartment together. As we moved down the hall, her demeanor shifted. When she opened the door to her bedroom, she could barely look at me. "It didn't used to be this way," Alaina murmured, wrapping herself in a blanket and sinking to the floor. "Mmm," was all I could say. I sat down beside her, leaning my back against the wall. At that moment, I wasn't sure I could help her. The bedroom was in worse shape than the communal spaces. I sensed that her letting go of the clutter was going to be difficult.

Alaina believed that by avoiding the unpacking, she would delay the reality of living somewhere she didn't love. But clutter, like unresolved emotions, only grows when it's ignored. Watching her struggle to commit to her home made me reflect on times I'd resisted settling in. I could remember feeling hesitant to fully unpack, fearing that embracing a space meant accepting a reality I wasn't ready for. Avoidance doesn't change a situation. It only prolongs discomfort. Whether we engage with our surroundings or we ignore them, they still shape us. The question is: Do we have the courage to shape them?

Alaina was rejecting a space she never chose. In doing so, she made it even harder to exist there. Sometimes, homemaking isn't about arranging furniture or organizing our belongings. It's the emotional work of accepting where we are in our lives, physically and emotionally. Letting go is about releasing fear, control, expectations, and outdated stories that keep us attached to things we neither want nor need. The more we resist, the more we cling to them—and the less space we have for what's next.

Making peace with a home, even one that isn't ideal, begins with a shift in perspective. Change requires action and acceptance. The first step toward decluttering is recognizing your power to shape your surroundings.

When Robert came home from work, he knocked on the bedroom door, peeking his head through the opening. "You see how we live?" he asked. He then led me through the boys' rooms and into his office. We sat across from each other at his desk.

"I've offered to help, but she won't let me," he admitted. "I asked if we could spend one day a week going through these boxes, but she says she'll get to it. When I try to start, she criticizes the way I'm doing it or takes over, then quits. Alaina says she wants help, but not from me. I don't want to live like this, but I don't know how to change it."

"What about your own stuff? Why not start there?" I asked.

"I could," he said.

Robert scheduled time with me to go through his belongings. We worked through his papers, electronics, and keepsakes. The boys followed his lead, setting aside toys and clothes they no longer wanted.

When they did that, Alaina became territorial. Every T-shirt, blanket, and trinket held a memory she wasn't ready to release. Every decision her family made about letting things go irritated her. Eventually, we had to cut the children's session short.

The clutter in their home wasn't because Alaina loved stuff. It was a silent protest. Every unopened box and untouched room was proof of Alaina's resistance. Letting go meant surrendering to the situation, and her resistance was a form of control. By keeping things in limbo, she was holding on to a fight she had already lost. The fight itself was what kept her disconnected.

Meanwhile, Robert wasn't waiting for perfect conditions for him to act. He knew the apartment was temporary and far from ideal. He also knew it was where they were now. He didn't see how engaging with the space was defeat. He wasn't waiting to feel good about the space before taking care of it. He was making it livable in the present.

Control and clutter go hand in hand. The more we try to control, the harder it is to change our surroundings. Alaina wasn't just holding on to things. She was also holding on to the idea that if she didn't oversee every decision, the home would evolve beyond her control. No matter what that evolution looked like, she was against it. For Alaina, her biggest obstacle was laying down the fight and choosing to live in the present.

Alaina would become my first client. Through our work together, we learned a lot about each other. We fought, laughed, cried, and, unknowingly, I began my career as a professional organizer. Serendipitously, her story became a part of my mine. If it had not been for Alaina, I would have never found the courage to leave my job at the restaurant and launch Organize With Faith.

One year later, Alaina and her family moved to another apartment, sending most of their boxes into storage. Although it didn't solve all their problems, it made the next place feel less cluttered.

A few years later, the family packed up that second apartment and moved to a large house on Long Island—along with the contents of their storage unit. Yearning to make the most of this new home, Alaina realized it was time to get to work. When I visited, every box was being unpacked. The boys set aside items they did not want, and Alaina did not protest. "I still keep some things," she joked as she taped her son's artwork onto the wall.

The house was coming together, and so was the family. A large part of their success was Alaina's acceptance that when other people help, they may not do things the way she would—but that's okay. A well-balanced home is a collaborative home. When we allow others to take ownership of their own spaces, we create space for ourselves as well. After all, if we don't let others try, how and when will they learn? The more Alaina let go of her expectation that she was solely responsible for the homemaking, the more her kids and husband could step in and contribute.

Alaina thought the key to a fresh start was to move somewhere new. In her case, that new house did make a big difference. However, moving to a new place doesn't erase old patterns. The real transformation happened not when she changed locations, but when she changed her mindset. She started self-reflecting to better understand her relationship to homemaking and housekeeping. She stopped resisting and started collaborating. Decluttering wasn't about losing the battle, but choosing what mattered most. The more she let go, the more at home she finally felt.

* * *

WATCHING ALAINA RELEASE her resistance, expectations, and need to control every detail caused me to reflect on my own relationship to home. I had never struggled with clutter in the way she did, but I knew what it was like to resist settling in. I also knew what it meant to hold on to something because I wasn't ready to face what would come next. We don't always love everything that we keep. Some things stay because we have yet to come to terms with what those things represent. Decluttering can be about surrendering a fight we didn't even realize we were in. It's acknowledging where we are, even when it's not where we thought we'd be. When we surrender, we aren't giving up. We're making room for something better.

A home is more than where we live. It's also *how* we live with ourselves and others. If we spend our time resisting, we will always feel unsettled. If we allow ourselves to engage with our space, to care for it as much as we care for those we love, we make something worth living in. We won't always get everything we want, or live in our dream home, but that doesn't mean we can't make the best of where we are. Never underestimate your ability to create change—to shape your space into something meaningful.

Decluttering isn't about making room for more things. It's about making space for more meaning in our lives. This housekeeping practice is for everyone, children included. Every item that stays with us carries a story. Every object we let go of frees us from something else. Every home we create is a reflection of not only who we are but also who we've been.

REFLECTIVE QUESTIONS

When thinking about your relationship to your home and your belongings, ask yourself:

- What am I holding on to that no longer serves me?
- What am I resisting? What do I feel the need to control?
- Is that control helping or hindering me?
- What am I creating space for?

As you answer these questions, reflect on the domestic models from your past. How have they shaped your ideas of homemaking? Identify the patterns you've inherited and ask yourself: Is it time to declutter?

Practical Steps for Letting Go

Acknowledge Your Resistance. Naming your resistance helps you understand what you're holding on to. Before decluttering, ask yourself: *If I stopped resisting, what would change?*

Shift from Control to Trust. As you reclaim your space, remain in the present. Make decisions that will alleviate clutter and ease mental or physical discomfort. Remember, things may not go as planned. If you feel discouraged, pause and remind yourself why you are decluttering and what you ultimately desire for your home.

Decide What's Worth Keeping. Instead of asking, "When was the last time I used this?", try, "What do I gain from keeping this? What do I gain from letting it go?"

Create Space for a New Way of Being. Letting go is about making intentional choices. It's not about what you release, but *why* you release it. Let the space you create reflect what supports you—emotionally, mentally, physically, and spiritually.

CHAPTER 4
ORGANIZE WITH FAITH

WHILE MY EARLY EXPERIENCE helping Alaina gave me confidence, my official introduction to professional organizing came via a woman named Vicky. She specialized in home organization and move management, and my friend Morgan was working for her part-time. When they needed extra assistance unpacking and organizing a house in the Hamptons, Morgan called me. Vicky, in her mid-fifties, wore crisp white shirts popped at the collar, her coiffed blond hair flipped up at her shoulders. She was empathetic, creative, and the ultimate people pleaser—the perfect combination for assisting anyone feeling lost, facing a life transition, or overwhelmed in crisis.

Vicky trained us to keep things light with clients. She joked that asking too many questions might open the door to intimate conversations that should take place in therapy. We were there to sort and organize their belongings. Our job was to box up the objects and take them to the basement, a closet, or a vacant room for the client to review in private. Vicky taught us small details, like arranging cups from smallest to tallest, which made opening a cabinet more pleasing to the eye. She demonstrated the KonMari fold before Marie Kondo came on the scene, but called it "the filing technique."

Morgan and I cherished these nuggets of wisdom, believing if we spent enough time in our wealthy clients' homes, we would absorb their luxurious lifestyle. Even though the money we were surrounded by was not ours, working in these homes helped fuel our fantasies. However, the life we thought we wanted was not what we imagined. Most of Vicky's clients weren't any happier because they had more money. It seemed the more we did for them, the less confidence they had in their ability to do things for themselves.

I was starting to think that even though we walked away from those projects with everything perfectly in place, we hadn't necessarily set the clients up for success. The psychological components for *keeping* a space organized were missing. Our services were superficial solutions. We organized without addressing the emotional attachments those clients had to their belongings—and their unresolved feelings were leading them to recurring clutter.

At first, Vicky's approach seemed logical: Keep things easy and efficient. We were always moving things from one place to another, from a closet to a basement, from an office to storage, but we were never addressing the root cause. We shielded people from both the discomfort and the growth that can come from making tough decisions. I started asking myself: *What are we accomplishing here?* More important, *what* is *organizing?*

Clients often attributed their clutter to external factors—demanding jobs, complex relationships, or familial obligations—seldom acknowledging their role in the mess. This deflection highlighted their resistance to confronting their personal attachments and emotions intertwined with their possessions. Some had given away objects and instantly regretted it, leading them to hold on to things rather than risk that feeling again. Others grew up with parents who tossed their stuff in the trash without their permission. Either way, the reasons for *not* decluttering were endless. And because they were endless and unclear, Vicky left the clients to sort things out on their own. Most of our jobs were straightforward—

organizing a kitchen or clearing out a closet. As we approached more complicated projects, I sensed the services Vicky offered were not enough.

* * *

JOE WAS AN OLD-SCHOOL NEW YORKER. He was seventy-eight, a straight shooter, and the father of one of Vicky's high-profile clients. Joe scored his SoHo apartment long before I was born. According to his son (who was footing the bill for our services), nothing had changed in the forty years he had lived there. Joe had accumulated a lifetime of stuff. Our job was to organize and pack up unnecessary belongings ahead of an upcoming renovation.

On the first day, we quietly went to Joe's office to sort through old paintings, outdated electronics, and papers on the verge of disintegration. On the second day, Morgan handled the bathrooms and I worked the hallway closet. I opened the door and ran my hand across coats of various hefts and lengths. Joe was over six feet tall. Two winter coats and one trench belonged to him, but the rest were for a much smaller woman. In fact, her coats consumed the closet, their pockets stuffed with napkins, MetroCards, ChapStick, and loose change.

"Are these Joan's?" I asked Morgan. Joe's partner, Joan, lived down the street and slept over on weekends. She had popped in a few times to encourage us as we sorted through Joe's clutter.

"They're his wife's," she replied.

"Wife?" I asked.

"Joe's wife, Vilma, died twelve years ago," Morgan replied.

I pointed toward the closet. It was more than a few coats. The closet was also packed with hats, boots, boxes of stationery, and purses. "This is all hers?" I asked.

"I think so," Morgan said.

Shortly after, Vicky walked by us, with her hand to her heart. She, too, was aware of Joe's twelve-year heartbreak. Vicky politely instructed us to move on to the next room, which stored more of the same. That night, I couldn't shake the feeling we'd missed something vital in Joe's home. I wondered what these things meant to him if Vilma no longer touched, wore, or owned them. Perhaps the purpose of keeping her things as they were was to capture his loss. Beyond that, my heart went out to his girlfriend. I hoped one day there would be enough space for her. I hoped she did not have to cram herself in between Joe, the memories of his late wife, and her possessions.

Joe's apartment was stuck in time. Although he wasn't living entirely in the past, he also wasn't fully in the present. Joe's choice to keep Vilma's things was him resisting a reality he was not ready to accept. Working with Joe helped me understand that objects hold emotions. We were boxing up Vilma's things to move them out of sight, yet they weren't gone. Joe's grief, his attachment, and his avoidance remained. Inside Joe's boxes were stories he wasn't ready to tell. Sometimes, things become placeholders for a meaningful moment in our lives. They can represent loss, regret, guilt, comfort, or hope.

When we hold on to certain objects, we hold on to who we once were. This realization made me question the work I had been doing with Vicky and underscored my growing conviction that organizing required confronting hard truths. I wanted to speak to Joe about his loss, but I couldn't. I wish I could have held space for him to tell his story. I wish I could have asked him questions that would help me understand what was holding him back. In that moment, I understood that if Joe could answer these questions, it would allow the organizing process to begin.

Joe's apartment was one of the last projects I would organize with Vicky, before I launched Organize With Faith, where confronting emotional truths would be central to the work. Joe's situation inspired me to pay attention to how much things can shift, yet still look the same.

As someone who processes my emotions through touch, my belongings have been the tools to help me reorient myself. In doing so, I've learned that a part of letting go is working through what those possessions represent. It's about recognizing the unconscious influences of objects upon our choices and actions. When I step into homes filled with people's pain, I know there is something else at play. I began to wonder: *Could I take what I know and use it to transform people's relationships with their homes?* In short, I wanted to help people the way I had helped myself.

* * *

I ASPIRED TO EMPOWER clients with the tools necessary for making lasting change. That represented the beginning of Soul Work, a holistic approach that delves into the psychological and emotional facets of decluttering, fostering genuine transformation beyond tidiness. My mindset was of the notion: Give a man a fish and you feed him for a day; teach a man to fish and you feed him for a lifetime. As I started taking on clients of my own, I noticed that most of them were calling for a quick fix. Professional organizers who do all the work were in high demand. As I gained more experience dealing with people, I understood why Vicky navigated her business the way she did. Soon, I too would keep quiet and not challenge clients' excuses in order to get the job done. My hope of empowering people to rethink their belongings as a tool to process difficult emotions was put on the back burner.

Vicky shared a few of her high-end clients with me, a generosity that positioned Organize With Faith as a top-tier service. Referrals kept coming in, and after each project, I would hire a photographer to shoot pictures of me in front of beautifully organized kitchens, closets, and playrooms. Afterward, I would post the photos on social media and on my website, which attracted journalists looking to interview organizing experts. Organize With Faith was featured in *The New York Times*, *Vogue*, *Bon Appétit*, *House Beautiful*, *Real Simple*, *Domino*, *Apartment Therapy*, *Epicurious*, and *Food and Wine*. It was exciting, but something was still troubling me.

I was selling a fantasy. My projects featured a specific clientele, a lifestyle I was groomed to produce and one to which I aspired myself. If a space failed to meet the prototype established by the domestic gurus, the client was unhappy. If a space did not live up to the examples on television or social media, people did not deem it "organized." Business kept coming in. By the end of my third year, I had five employees. I taught these employees the beauty in the details, organizing clothes from lightest to darkest, unboxing cans of soda and spacing them meticulously on the shelf, folding one shirt on top of another to ensure they are the same width. They learned how to elevate a space to such a high standard that only a professional could maintain it.

Throughout those years, I worked alongside a few clients who did express a desire for a more personal and heartfelt organizing approach. I relished those opportunities, encouraging people to explore their home history and their relationship to their belongings, alongside their values and life purpose. I questioned their perceptions about their habits and sense of self-worth. We focused on their ability to energetically sort through the shadows that were stifling their potential for growth.

Traditional home organizing tells us to focus on aesthetics, on making a space look good. Soul Work is about personal transformation. It's about understanding who you are and what truly matters to you. Soul Work prepares you to declutter—it primes you to let go.

The more insight you have, the easier it is to release. Soul Work is introspection. If decluttering is the letting go, Soul Work is the *why* behind it.

At its core, Soul Work is rooted in truth—being honest with ourselves about what we're holding on to. It requires patience—knowing that this process will take us time. It calls for self-acceptance—releasing the idea that our homes (or we) have to be perfect. This inquiry of the self asks us to slow down and trust in the unknown.

The biggest difference between Soul Work and traditional decluttering and organizing is this: Soul Work does not rely on creating a fantasy or perfection. It's not about clearing space to "get organized." It's about honing a relationship with yourself, engaging in dialogue to understand yourself better. It's the act of reclaiming your space as a reflection of *who you are now*, not who you used to be or who you want to be. Soul Work is about self-care. This is what was missing when I focused solely on organization and appearance.

* * *

IT'S IMPORTANT TO NOTE THIS: Soul Work is not something you do once and never have to do again. It's a practice that reveals a commitment to yourself. Our lives are constantly changing, as are we. Soul Work grounds us at those different stages of our lives. When we refuse to take the time to understand what we're feeling, decluttering can seem impossible to do. If the idea of letting go is daunting, or the thought of organizing your home makes you freeze, you need to start with Soul Work.

We all have stories, histories, and beliefs that create blind spots. When we can't fully see what we're capable of achieving, or what we're missing, Soul Work guides us. When we hold space for ourselves to organize our thoughts and feelings, letting go of things becomes easier.

The results are not flashy, yet something extraordinary is accomplished with Soul Work. By the end of the process, clients who choose to participate will have strengthened their capacity to be self-reliant. The clarity that develops through our work together allows them to create an authentic space. After I leave those clients on their own, they continue to report progress, further enhancing their spaces as their skills develop even more and their confidence increases.

Unfortunately, these models were few and far between.

* * *

ONE WINTER DAY, a client I had been working with over the past year said, “Faith, I received your Christmas card in the mail—beautiful—but you are not that type of organizer.” The card to which he was referring looked like an advertisement for organizing products. It pictured a bright white pantry loaded with jars decanted with dried foods, and wicker baskets with cursive labels. I’d thought this showed the caliber of styling for which Organize With Faith had become known, but it failed to capture the work I was doing with this particular client.

His comment stayed with me. The next morning, I called my former roommate, pal, and handyman Tim to help me investigate why.

“Tim, do you think Organize With Faith represents me?” I asked.

“No. But is it supposed to? Your social media represents your clientele and all the fabulous homes you organize. Right?”

“Right!” I agreed.

“I mean, when I look at your Instagram,” Tim continued, “I don’t get a sense of who you are or what you believe, if that’s what you’re asking.”

Hmm. There was a big contrast between what I had hoped for my company to be and the services I was actually providing. This sent me on a mission to figure out what I believed to be true about making a home. I had tested many of the well-known methods prescribed by the industry. After watching *The Minimalist* documentary, I obediently disposed of my excess Christmas ornaments, curtains, unused kitchen appliances, and an area rug. I sat on a chair in the middle of a living room so bare it echoed. However, having less did not make me feel like I had more. Living minimally did not make me happier. I was not suddenly experiencing a more adventurous life because my living room had only two chairs in it.

I then pivoted to the KonMari method. A cheerful, tidy house decorated with only objects that sparked joy was not sustainable. Pretty soon the relevance of those objects would fade into the background of what mattered most—my well-being. After that, I went to the Container Store and treated myself to a shopping spree. Spending an unnecessary amount of money on containers and trekking back to my apartment with my purchases made me feel surprisingly productive. I was already organized—my things were where I liked them—but putting them in containers showed off my expertise. After assembling everything, my closets and drawers looked more uniform and polished, though the maintenance was a pain. Decanting my smoothie powders and nuts into glass jars occupied more of my time than I wanted to give.

Even though my home was neat, there were days when I was not in love with my space. Having tried all the commercial methods for obtaining domestic bliss, what kept me most engaged was thinking of decluttering and tidying up as a way to gain a new perspective on my life. Checking in with my feelings and gaining a better understanding of myself were the only rewards I was truly willing to work for.

One night while staying at a client's house during a big organizing project, I was unable to sleep. I kept thinking of my most successful projects. These were when clients told me about their values, their personal history, and their purpose in organizing. I realized that equipping people with the techniques that probed self-inquiry opened the door to authenticity.

That night, I began researching life-coaching programs. Becoming a life coach helped me shift the tone of Organize With Faith's practice. Soon I began attracting clients interested in using a holistic perspective to let go. I encouraged clients to organize their spaces to support their mental, emotional, and spiritual growth, while eschewing the burden of perfection. Even if they did not always have the answers, the questions they asked themselves would challenge their perceptions of space and their responsibilities.

Soul Work sessions became the catalyst for personal transformation. Through their introspective decluttering, clients not only organized their spaces but also confronted and released their emotional burdens, paving the way to renewed clarity and purpose. Throughout our sessions, the clients would review their decisions and reflect on their life journey, ultimately releasing their resistance to the unknown and welcoming change in their homes and within themselves.

For a while, I did Soul Work with a few people while continuing to work as an organizer who still delivered perfection to other clients. But Soul Work attracted new clients: We were hired by tenants on the verge of eviction and seniors disqualified from receiving home health aides because of the state of their homes. Family members clearing the estates of loved ones and people with restricted mobility who could not physically housekeep themselves called us in need. For these clients, decluttering and organizing was not a luxury. It was a necessity, and Soul Work was absolutely vital to it.

Some clients had such an abundance of stuff that it sucked the life out of their homes. Tunnels were burrowed through their stuff, which then dictated where they could go in their apartments. I began asking questions whenever someone wanted to hire us in order to gauge the client's state of mind.

- How long have you been living with this clutter?
- What has stood in the way of you living differently?
- Why do you want to make this change now?
- What are you looking to learn from this process?
- On a scale of from 1 to 10, how difficult is it to let ___ go?

That difficult-to-release item could be books, clothes, papers—whatever was crowding them out. Most people would say they were anywhere between a 5 and a 7 on the scale. A score of 10 was for those who would put up a fight. Once we started the decluttering, it would sometimes become clear that the client's much higher. Having an excessive attachment to things promotes the idea that things matter more than we do. In reality, we bring those items to life.

There is a big difference between doing something for someone when it is a luxury versus a necessity. It's a luxury when someone hires me to make a closet look pretty, when we're matching baskets to wallpaper and measuring drawers for tiny acrylic containers. It's a necessity when a person has neglected their well-being in favor of inanimate objects, or when a client cannot decide between their livelihood and the clutter.

There is also the middle ground, where we all meet—the point at which we have to decide if our things matter more to us than our peace of mind.

* * *

SOUL WORK AND DECLUTTERING aren't linear motions. While Soul Work often comes before decluttering, you don't always have to do one before the other. Sometimes, emotional work pops up in the middle of the decluttering. One day, you might find yourself crying into a bin of old birthday cards. Or, you'll reach into a drawer, touch something, and suddenly feel unsure, overwhelmed, or stuck in time. That's your signal. That moment of hesitation is a compass, pointing you inward.

Decluttering itself can become Soul Work when it stirs up memories, beliefs, or values you haven't questioned in a while. When something feels sticky, don't push past it. Pause. Ask yourself, *Why is this hard to let go? What does this represent? What am I afraid to lose—or admit?*

In those moments, the line between Soul Work and letting go is fluid. That fluid zone is where personal transformation lives.

REFLECTIVE QUESTIONS

When it comes to getting organized, Soul Work and decluttering are key to the process. When you consider tidying up, ask yourself:

- What is driving my desire to get organized?
- Which aspects of getting organized feel like a luxury to me? Which feel like a necessity?
- What organizing methods have I tried before? Have they addressed my emotional needs?
- What kind of support do I truly need for meaningful, lasting change?

CHAPTER 5

THE HEART OF THE MATTER

MY FATHER SUGGESTED it might be time to move. He was visiting from California, watching me as I puttered around the Washington Heights apartment where I had been living for a decade. He reminded me of the dorm shuffle at the Roanoke commune.

"Not good to get too comfortable . . ."

After his visit, I obsessed over the self-growth a move might invite. I dreamed of springing from my apartment of ten years into a shiny new development downtown. I imagined waking up to views of the city, waving to the doorman on my way out, leaving my dishes in the sink for someone else to clean, and choosing what to wear from a wardrobe of silk and cashmere. I adopted a mantra that I chanted with my friends: "Let me come up with the money for the land of milk and honey."

I thought my hard work might have more meaning if I came home to a place that was high in the sky. With each new client, I raised my prices, holding my breath every time I jumped another twenty-five dollars. I knew the land of milk and honey would be worth every cent—the space would be modern, minimal, and everything brand-new. Once I had a little more cash in my pocket, I focused on a new development in Long Island City. Construction was still underway, so the Realtor showed me a staged studio apartment that was a replica of my floor plan. I applied for a lease on the spot.

My mother, homemaker extraordinaire, hopped on a plane from California to help me move. Her visit would be the first time we slept under the same roof since I was sixteen years old. Once we were in the Washington Heights apartment together, our troubled history resurfaced. Like muscle memory, we began arguing. The fight was over whether the wooden folding chairs in my living room were attractive or not. I defended the chairs with a fervor that took effort, given I'd picked them up from an estate clearing years ago. Further, what I was defending was my right to choose what defined my home. Had any friend made the same comment, I would have laughed it off, but from my mother, the critique felt like a rejection of the life I'd painstakingly built.

I left the apartment to cool off. To my surprise, I came back to an apology. She didn't apologize for the chairs, or even for our argument. She apologized for the heart of the matter. For the years of silence after I left home at sixteen. For holding on too tightly. For not knowing how to bridge the gap between us, and letting pride and hurt keep us apart. Her admission softened something deep within me—an inner hardness I hadn't known was there. For the first time, I could grieve with her. She gave me what I didn't realize I had wanted: recognition that my pain was real, valid, and shared.

There is a saying, "You repeat what you don't repair." For most of my twenties, Mama and I were on repeat. As I got older, I came to realize she was more than my mother. She was a woman who'd experienced trauma. On this day, she shined a light on the season of our lives that was filled with sadness. Together, we healed.

After that, we settled into a companionable silence as she sewed cushions for the bench in my new foyer. We sorted through my belongings. I donated hand-me-downs because none of them were good enough for where I was headed. I kept only a few irreplaceable keepsakes. We made a mobile out of broken necklaces I could not bear to part with. We picked up boxes from Home Depot, and I reserved the new building's elevator for moving day.

This new building was impressive, fully equipped with a gym, pool, outdoor movie theater, heated floors, and floor-to-ceiling windows. My apartment was on the sixteenth floor. I had come a long way from my quirky Washington Heights flat. Still, I was not prepared for what the transition would bring up emotionally. As I began unpacking, an unexpected sorrow enveloped me. There, nestled in cardboard boxes, were my most cherished memories. A menagerie of objects that recounted my life and evolution, items infused with my identity. Hats my grandmother knitted that comforted me now that she had passed. Silver swan salt-and-pepper shakers my mother and I found at a flea market that were symbolic of rare peaceful afternoons. An embroidered Christmas stocking from Keith's mother, a reminder of a path I almost took.

My mother insisted we unpack every box that first night. Her excitement couldn't be contained. "Are you happy?" she asked, as I broke down boxes.

"I guess," I replied reluctantly.

"You look like you're in shock." The city lights twinkled outside the window. I didn't answer.

My mom flew back to California three days later, and I struggled to feel at home in my new place. I hired a feng shui consultant to help me balance the *qi* in the apartment. I organized the cabinets and closets to perfection, but for months I slept on a mattress on the floor. "I can't choose a headboard," I told my mother over the phone.

"At least get a bed frame!" she replied.

"There are so many windows in here. I feel like I'm living in a fish bowl," I said.

"You're sleeping on the floor, Faith. Order a bed frame," she insisted before we said goodbye.

I sat for a moment on a beautiful copper stool at the spotless kitchen counter. Above my head danced my old jewelry. I had imagined a life of luxury and freedom. Yet, once I was there, the emptiness felt like confinement, revealing how much my sense of home depended *not* on ease but on emotional connection.

Every fiber of my being wanted to relish my success, yet something felt off. I walked around the apartment and touched old belongings standing out against a fantasy that felt foolish now. I stared at myself in the mirror as I reminisced about my childhood and how far I had come. In my reflection, I saw my mother and her mother standing in an unfamiliar space. For the first time since I had moved to New York City, I was homesick for California.

I'd lived with my mother's rigid expectations at home, but there had been a sense of familiarity. Granny's apartment had been small, but it held love. Roanoke had been temporary, but it offered purpose. Here, surrounded by luxury, I was confronting not feeling at home in the space that I chose.

I missed the keepers of the places I inhabited while growing up. Their steady hands, comforting routines, and quiet strength had turned ordinary spaces into sanctuaries. I craved their integrity, and I longed for their example. I had promised myself the day I moved to New York that my home would be like my auntie's—always open for anyone to visit. Now, I lived in a 500-square-foot studio with barely enough room for me, let alone guests.

I missed my old apartment. I missed the kitchen grout stained from too much cooking and the dim light peeking through the ground-floor windows. I missed the duvet cover softened from relentless washing and the couch worn from the weight of visitors. Without these things present, I struggled to feel at home. I had let so many things go before the move that there was barely anything left to ground me. What I did bring with me were small reminders of a life I once lived and of the person I used to be.

At that moment, the objects I had preserved adopted new meaning. They became anchors to my past life. My anxiety about losing my identity revealed why decluttering is a challenge. I felt I had released the physical proof of who I once was. I felt as if a part of me had died. My history was entangled in those belongings. I grieved the realization that I could no longer revisit items that represented my quest for a stable home—the dinner parties, the botched engagement, and the growth of my business. Over time, I recognized that the version of myself I feared losing was that very part of myself that needed to evolve. The space created by decluttering (albeit scary) became an opportunity to reframe my story and redefine my life.

* * *

ONE EMOTION THAT frequently emerges in Soul Work is regret. In my case, regret wasn't merely nostalgia, it was also fear disguised as longing for what I'd given away—the comfort of a space and belongings that held memories of my past. The absence of these physical reminders forced me to confront the unknown future I'd stepped into. My regret in letting go was actually my fear of moving forward.

Regret is also profound in objects we do not want but refuse to release—the products of wishes unfulfilled, opportunities missed, or moments we yearn to rewrite. Interestingly, the regret we are trying to avoid by ignoring these things is often what we end up experiencing. We still encounter the tension, the frustration, the wanting to do things differently. When we are not content with our space, the internal conflict we feel is the very thing we've been trying to avoid by holding on. As regret grows beyond the fear of making the wrong decision, we live with the reality of what happens when we *don't* make a decision. The choice *not* made is as much a harbinger of regret as that of making a regrettable decision. The things we don't do, and the opportunities we don't take, are scientifically proven to be what plague us most.

Feelings of regret present a profound opportunity to confront what we fear and transform it into growth. When we reframe regret as a moment to reexamine our lives and chart our new course, we ignite a fire within, informing us of the parts of ourselves that need attention. Therefore, decluttering fearlessly outweighs whatever wrong decisions you might anticipate. The road to getting what you want will inevitably produce some mistakes, but that does not mean the road is not worth taking.

As we change, our relationship to things does too. How we live, where we live, what we like, all this is up for review as we prepare for a new season of life. As we grow out of love for certain objects, we release them. The space that we create through this process can feel like a loss, but what we've made is room to grow. Growth can be intimidating and seem out of our control. However, if we are clear about our intentions and our hopes for our future, we have a greater chance of growing toward reaching our goals. When it's time to release the objects of our past, rather than fear the unknown, let's think about holding the newfound space for a future to be born.

Our possessions are a means of self-expression. We rely on our belongings to affirm our existence, to mark our survival. Sometimes, however, we forget that we are also the evidence of our existence. The forces that define our character aren't found in our objects but, rather, within ourselves. Possessions cannot fulfill the part of ourselves that only we can express.

Anticipate regret on this decluttering journey. As we go through our home deciding what to keep and what to let go, we'll find all sorts of memories will arise. Some memories will be tethered to feelings of regret. We use these memories as data to help us reshape or reimagine our life. Overcoming regret requires releasing the limiting beliefs about ourselves and our past, and creating space to embrace the potential that awaits us.

* * *

I ONCE HEARD A SAYING that went something like, "If you are standing in the light, you will see your shadow." That is, if we observe our actions and thoughts closely, we will find flaws. We might not like what we see. Our responsibility is not to shrink into the shadows but, rather, to remain in the light. It's to take our regrets and learn from them. These moments help shape a present of which we can be proud. I assure you that our purpose is not to wallow in our mistakes or to be paralyzed by the fear of making mistakes. Rather, it is to live compassionately toward ourselves and others. If compassion is our intent, then regret becomes a valuable teacher.

REFLECTIVE QUESTIONS

As you explore the feeling of regret, practice cultivating compassion for your past and present self.

- Have you noticed anything in your home that stirs up feelings of regret?
- If a fear of regret arises, what's your worst imagined scenario and how could you realistically recover if it came true?
- How specifically has this fear prevented you from fully stepping into the home and life you envision?
- How might your life shift if you choose faith over fear?
- If an object evokes a regretful memory, pause and reflect: *What were the circumstances at that time?* Consider

your knowledge, emotional state, age, and environmental influences. How did these factors influence your decision?

- How can you extend empathy to your past self, recognizing that you made decisions based on what you knew and felt at that moment?

CHAPTER 6

MAKING SPACE FOR GRACE

WHEN I MET MONIQUE, she had already downsized her life significantly. She hired me to help her go further. To do this, we opened a discussion about her past and her desires for the present. Twice a week, we would meet at 5:30 a.m. in an empty apartment on the Upper West Side. This apartment would eventually become her new home. At the time, Monique lived in a larger apartment in the same building a few flights up.

Since there was nothing in the new space except two chairs, all we could do was talk about her life, the lessons she had learned, and her intentions for this apartment. Monique's top priority was clarity, and together we were organizing her mind. Retired, no longer married, and her children now adults, Monique found herself craving a different lifestyle.

Most mornings, we focused on refining her intentions to determine what objects she wanted to bring into this new space. Other days, we discussed the mental and emotional clutter clouding her judgment, enticing her to cling to an outdated version of herself. Monique had spent decades building a lifestyle she assumed she wanted, one she thought people expected of her. The more money Monique made, the grander her life became. The more she acquired, the more people she hired. Her lifestyle soon grew beyond what she truly wanted.

Speaking of summers on her yacht, Monique said, "I was

on the boat, but *I* wasn't really *on* the boat." She was physically present, although mentally somewhere else—disconnected from the woman she knew herself to be. That woman didn't crave extravagance. She craved freedom. Monique longed for a life of simplicity—free not only from the burden of things but also the expectations they carried. Monique's clarity of purpose helped point me in a new direction.

Our identity is often tied to our possessions: The clothes we wear, the homes we live in, the cars we drive, the objects we collect—these things speak for us. They are symbols, and sometimes they tell a story that isn't ours. The more we acquire, the easier it becomes to forget who we are beneath it all.

As my business got busier and I was making a decent living, wealth became the framework for my life. My aspirations had nothing to do with who I was, but everything to do with who I believed I should be. Everything I had chosen, from the apartment itself to the objects within it, were there to make me feel rich. But when guests left, I felt physically exhausted. Maintaining the illusion of perfection left me anxious, never truly at rest. Despite having a beautifully curated home, I often went to bed feeling disconnected from my life.

My fantasy was constructed with precision. I purposefully closed the door on anything that might have grounded me in reality. I hid the ugly evidence of chores or responsibilities because my luxurious lifestyle could not be bogged down by housekeeping. Dish sponges went under the sink, soap was decanted in decorative dispensers (concealing my domestic labor). Every surface was neat, yet I found myself pacing restlessly, unable to settle into a life that felt increasingly confined. I tidied with urgency to prove to myself and to others that I was worthy of what I had created.

Witnessing Monique's clarity helped illuminate my misplaced

motivations, prompting an honest examination of the life I had been crafting. As much as I enjoyed visiting clients who lived in penthouses with panoramic views, I decided my fancy studio was no longer my dream apartment. I now knew that domestic perfection was not my ticket to happiness, nor was it my measure of success.

When we reevaluate our motivations for wanting an organized home, and we take time to question our intentions, we quiet the distractions that prevent us from recognizing what we actually need. A housekeeping approach centered on our core values, not on the display of our possessions, is key here. I have tried *many* popular organizing methods, and I have found that nothing works better than organizing around *passion*, *purpose*, and *self-care*.

My *passion* for cooking energizes and nourishes me. My kitchen is decluttered and organized to support culinary creativity and to ensure that nothing goes to waste. My *purpose* is to uplift myself and others. A tidy and inviting home allows me to comfortably welcome friends who, like me, are also seeking connection. Practicing *self-care* means I cultivate a place to recharge, keeping only what genuinely supports my well-being. When I keep those values front of mind, housekeeping doesn't feel burdensome.

Ultimately, every home I have made gives me new information and offers a chance to try something new. The systems I create are easier to maintain when they are built with intention. Each one of us holds the data we need to create a space that makes sense for who we are. I take everything I am—the obstacles I have overcome, how I was brought up, my work ethic, my relationships—and I build a home centered on my whole self. The more familiar I am with my life experiences, the more equipped I am to know what I need.

My job is to support you as you build a space representing your authentic self. It is to challenge what you say you want, and to test whether this aligns with who you say you are. At Organize With

Faith, I say, "Tell me who you are. Tell me what your core values are. How do your values translate into how you keep house? How do you treat yourself and others in your space?" These prompts underlie the driving force in your life, which will carry you through the difficulties you will face when you start to declutter. You have to know who you are to eliminate what you are not. Monique's desire to simplify her life forced me to confront my reasons for choosing luxury. Her realization about her yacht inspired me to look at my notions of perfection and success.

* * *

LYNN'S FAITH IN GOD is a core value for her. At seventy years old, her days are organized around taking walks with girlfriends, studying the Bible with fellow church members, and meditating at a local Buddhist temple. One of the first things Lynn shared with me was the grief she felt about the tumultuous relationship she had with her daughter and son. Her resistance to clearing out the clutter in her apartment had pushed her children away. After countless arguments, they gave her a choice: She had to either ditch the clutter or lose her connection to her family. "They feel that I love my things more than I do them. That is not true, but they are not here. My things are all I have, and God, of course," she said.

I was called in because Lynn would be evicted if she did not clean up her apartment. A red sign was pasted to her apartment door, stating the number of days she had to clear her space. When I spoke to Lynn on the phone, she had not mentioned the sign. On the day she greeted me at the door, she pointed to it and said, "How cruel is this? And I am not allowed to remove it." Lynn seemed more agitated by the display on her front door than the ramifications of her not clearing out her clutter. She had two weeks to get her house in order. Surprisingly, the eviction notice and the children's ultimatum weren't what motivated Lynn. Her true desire was to host gatherings for her spiritual community.

While we walked together through her apartment, Lynn described her challenges when she attempted to declutter: the lack of motivation or resources to get assistance, her physical ailments, and the mental fatigue. She had tucked away a small table in the corner of her living room that was draped in a pink silk cloth. The table held pictures, sacred scripts, and a tiny Buddha statue. When we approached the altar, she beamed with pride. Amid her clutter, she had carved a path for spiritual enlightenment. Lynn had discovered Buddhism in her late sixties, and had found that it aligned with her Christianity.

Lynn expressed her gratitude for the Buddhist community to which she belonged. "They saved my life. They accept me the way I am." Every week a friend from the temple hosted a meditation session at their home. Lynn wanted to do the same, but was caught in a dilemma—no one could comfortably fit into her apartment because the place was so crammed with stuff.

"This is not what God would want for me," Lynn said. She recognized the contradiction between how she lived and what she believed. Her goal was to create a space that supported her beliefs and enriched her life. It was her values that motivated her to slowly begin to do what at first seemed impossible. Her determination to persist despite her challenges was connected to her faith.

Lynn had lived for years in a space that divided her from her family, ostracized her from her friends, and dimmed her light. To Lynn, enriching her religious practice meant opening her home. The difficulty was no longer a personal obstacle. It was a spiritual one that made her Soul Work worth doing.

* * *

EACH DAY, our beliefs shape our thoughts, actions, and speech. Our values are often present when we make life-affirming decisions, whether to go to church, volunteer our services, or attend marches. The same should be true when we approach homemaking. Housekeeping, decluttering, and organizing take on a different meaning when we are clear about the reasons we are doing them. The focus is not on the outcome but on the process.

In engaging with the part of ourselves that strives to meet our highest potential, we must reflect on why we live the way we do. With an awareness of who we are and what we believe, we can open a dialogue between ourselves and our domestic space. Knowing what values to bring forth to help release the possessions that are getting in our way is key to making that space.

When clients feel out of alignment with their homes, I apply this technique to help them recenter themselves. First, we acknowledge the values that are essential to them. Using Lynn as an example, I noted that her core value is her spirituality. Then, we identify a domestic action that exercises that value. For instance, decluttering Lynn's space was a domestic action that helped her practice Christ's example of how to handle material possessions. Lastly, we create a statement that recognizes the connection between our values and our home. This statement is then repeated as we build a space that supports our well-being. For example, Lynn's statement was something like, "As I release the possessions that clutter my home, I make space for others and for myself to freely worship God."

By identifying a value, linking it to explicit domestic actions, and creating a clear affirmation, we can develop direction to guide ourselves to meaningful and lasting change.

* * *

HERE IS ANOTHER EXAMPLE, where the value is *simplicity*.

Step 1: Acknowledgment (Acknowledge a value.) *Simplicity is important to me.*

Step 2: Action (Give an example of a domestic action that supports or exercises your value.) *Decluttering things that get in my way or make my life unnecessarily complicated.*

Step 3: Alignment (Make a simple statement combining the first two steps.) *I align with simplicity by releasing thoughts, behaviors, and objects that unnecessarily complicate my life.*

If I performed this exercise for *peace,* which is a value of mine, I would say the following:

Step 1: Acknowledgment (Acknowledge a value.) *Peace is important to me.*

Step 2: Action (Give an example of a domestic action that supports or exercises your value.) *Keeping my living room floor clear as a space to stretch my body. Keeping my bedroom clean so I can meditate before bed.*

Step 3: Alignment (Make a simple statement combining the first two steps.) *I align with peace when I clear spaces to physically and mentally nurture myself.*

Decluttering and organizing our possessions helps us reflect on our choices. Dissatisfaction ensues when our domestic actions and values are not in sync—when our core values are compromised.

When this disconnect happens, our way of living is not in alignment with our beliefs. Realigning ourselves with our space takes more than just shifting things around. It's not about thanking your socks or expressing gratitude to your house for protecting you. It's about seeing yourself from a different point of view. It's also not about how much things cost or what containers to keep markers in. It's about learning how to approach each setting to get the most out of our lives.

We do not always know what we want or understand what truly makes us happy. However, orienting ourselves around our values makes letting go a little bit easier. There is so much more to life than what we own. There is so much more to homemaking than what we have. Let your values, not your valuables, be what shapes your home.

* * *

MOTIVES ARE CRITICAL to realizing our dreams. They are the compass that helps us chart our course. If we do not understand our motivations, we risk the mistake of creating an inauthentic home. What is our motivation for having a tidy home? Is our motivation in alignment with our values? What do we stand for and how is that reflected in our homemaking and housekeeping? These are the key questions to answer.

Some organizers start with aesthetics, which is an outside-in approach that often skips over the internal alignment that is so necessary. I admit that presentation has always been important to me. I am invested in how spaces look, feel, and evolve over time. However, when we focus solely on the aesthetics, we are perpetuating a false hope that everything will simply fall into place.

Another narrative that appears is that if your home is a mess, so are you. Yet I have seen people who were internally chaotic, living in the tidiest spaces. I have also worked with people who think as clearly as a bell, even though their apartments are a mess. No matter which way the pendulum swings, how things look on the outside is not a measure of who we are on the inside. Our home is a reflection of what we value.

If you are unhappy with your space, then now is the time to bring your values to the fore. Feel free to reassess them, because what you prioritized in your youth may not be what you need or want as you mature. Identifying what is essential will help center you as you work to transform your home. Whether your priorities are family, community, spiritual growth, or physical health, your responsibility is to make a home that supports your values and, in turn, supports your needs.

Look around your house and take in the environment you have created. Remember that what you bring into your space either uplifts your values or diminishes them. Is this how you want to live? Think of clearing out the pollution in your home as a way to dust off your principles and foster a purpose-filled life. Remember, we are not going for perfection here. We are identifying emotional, mental, and spiritual value. We are making space for grace.

REFLECTIVE QUESTIONS

When you think of your values in relation to your home, ask yourself:

- What are my core values?
- In what ways do I see those values being lived out in my home?

- Which of these values have I neglected to practice at home?
- What difference could nurturing these values make in my life?
- Is there a value I have held on to that no longer serves me? What might I replace it with?

CHAPTER 7

AN ONGOING JOURNEY

AFTER A COUPLE OF YEARS in my dream high-rise that never quite felt like home, I longed for life back at street level—where neighbors chatted on street corners and local grocers knew your name. I wanted the warmth of Washington Heights wrapped in the quaintness of Queens.

The apartment I had my eye on was off the market, but I knew the unit was available. I used to work for the owner of the building, Coco, often walking the mile there from my studio. Her two-family brick house had a garden flourishing in the front yard. One day, I made a surprising discovery: The house had an entire apartment downstairs. When we were looking for financial documents, Coco asked me to search a filing cabinet in the basement. To get there, I had to go down a flight of stairs. It was then that I discovered the two-bedroom apartment with a backyard, and a washer and dryer. This apartment was gold, but had been vacant for years.

When Coco didn't return my calls, I rode my bike over to her place and chucked pebbles at the second-floor window to get her attention. Coco was in her late seventies and lived alone. She had no children, smoked like a chimney, and never left her recliner, which was right next to her phone. I knew this move could benefit us both.

I waited outside, singing her name until she opened the window in her nightgown. Coco explained that she had not been feeling well. She assumed I was calling to see if she needed maintenance on the organizing we had done last year. After her husband, Roger, got sick and moved to an assisted-living facility, she was inundated with bills, so she had hired me to organize the mail.

I explained I was really there to see if she might let me rent the downstairs apartment.

"Faith, no one has lived down there for years. And it's filled with Roger's papers."

"I know, I've seen it. But I can help."

"Why don't you come spend the night to see if you really want to do this."

"Sure," I agreed.

When I arrived for the overnight, Coco was waiting at the front door. "It takes a while for me to get down the stairs, so I gave myself a head start. Come on in." The apartment looked abandoned. Furniture was scattered around the room as if someone had decorated in the dark. It had been nicer in my imagination. The house was old, the ceiling tiles bowed from years of humidity, and the laminate floors and kitchen cabinets had turned yellow over time. The whole place smelled of cigarette smoke, seeping in through the ceiling that divided the two apartments.

Later that night, unable to sleep, I called my mother.

"I don't think I can do this," I whispered.

"What do you mean?"

"I feel like I know too much about the person who lived here before me. I mean, I don't *know* him, but I feel like I'm getting to know him and it's a lot."

"But don't you like her?" my mother asked.

"I do, she's a sweetheart. Mom, part of the deal of me moving in would be to help her go through the apartment to get rid of her husband's stuff. There's a lot to unpack, and she wants to tell me stories that I don't want to know," I said.

"You can do it!" Mom said.

I hung up the phone and turned off the light. Before drawing the curtains, I cracked the window for some air. The room was silent, there were no sounds from the city streets or lights from the buildings next door. As I laid there in the quiet, something within me shifted. It wasn't the silence of loneliness but, rather, that of possibility. I had the power to transform this space, physically and energetically. I could make it my own. With that thought, I could finally fall asleep. The next morning, I woke to the songs of birds.

For the next two months, Coco and I met three days a week to declutter the apartment. Beyond decluttering, we also renovated the bathroom and kitchen, and replaced the ceilings. As the weeks passed, I created task lists that we could work on both together and independently to ensure the place was on track for my move-in date. We used the apartment's living room as a temporary holding space for things Coco wanted to keep. From there, we focused on one room at a time. This part is always a bit of a dance, as different spaces hold things that require different actions.

To keep decluttering projects moving, I schedule services before I'm fully ready—junk haulers, cleaners, shredders—using their deadlines as my motivation. Worst case, I reschedule. Best case, progress is made. My goal is to make the decluttering experience reluctance-free. The best way to do this is to have people in line who can debunk any fallacies. For instance, I call in a local appraiser when clients think their objects are of significant financial value. People often overestimate the value of things and hold on to them for this reason. To nip all that guessing in the bud, I invite the expert to tell us what things are worth. If there's not much money attached, then we can declutter with more ease. The same goes for papers. Clients are more likely to declutter their personal papers when they know they are going to be shredded. Information is liberation: The more you know, the easier it will be to let things go.

Coco and I did not have the first problem because Roger did not own anything we could sell. Nevertheless, every room was filled with stuff. The most efficient way to declutter is by category, but when a space is maxed out, the thought of gathering all the books in one spot, or all the keepsakes in another area, is nearly impossible. To create some wiggle room, we needed to first take out the trash. Bagging up the trash, taking out the empty boxes, recycling materials, and sorting the junk mail, empty soda cans, and used paper plates yields significant results. You might be surprised at how much space you can create when you take out the trash.

We finished clearing out and renovating the apartment in February 2020. Ultimately, the timing of my move was perfect. Within a few weeks, the city would be shut down due to the pandemic. I was grateful to be quarantined in a two-bedroom apartment with a backyard. I felt a quiet pride as I stood in my new place. I realized I had crafted a home true to myself. For the first time, my living space aligned completely with who I was, and I could finally exhale. Coco was right. The apartment was not fancy like the high-rise I had lived in, but neither was I.

Before moving to Queens, I donated many of my things. This time, I wasn't letting go in anticipation of who I wanted to become. Instead, I was shedding the version of myself I once felt I had to be. I had lived in New York City for eighteen years, and that entire time I'd been trying to reinvent myself as Faith 2.0. Designing my new home with loving attention and care, I learned to appreciate the imperfections and quirks in every room, as well as those within myself. What would have bothered me about the new place ten years ago I now viewed as part of its history. The key to contentment in a space (that is not necessarily Instagrammable or a complete disaster) is to ask yourself what brings meaning to your life, and is it reflected in your space. This beauty will not be the type that fades. It will evolve as you pursue a deeper relationship with yourself.

* * *

ONE YEAR LATER, I felt happy in my apartment, my business was moving along, and I found myself craving adventure. For the first time, I was in a home that reflected who I was, not who I thought I needed to be. With that clarity, I was ready to take a leap into something new. I would finally explore a quiet yearning within me: country living. On a whim, I bought my first property, a log cabin upstate, along with a 1989 blue pickup truck that I named Babe. An apartment in the city would have been a better financial investment, but I wanted a place that reminded me of my childhood in California. I was craving the days spent at my grandparents' home near the lake.

When my realtor first showed me the cabin, I was not exactly impressed. The exterior logs were painted the color of khaki pants and the entire house was hidden behind overgrown trees that made it easy to miss. One thing you could not miss, however, were the fake flowers stuck in the dirt of the front yard. The owners suggested I go check out the dock. The lake was still that day, and there was not a cloud in the sky. As I sat in an Adirondack chair, a great blue heron flew overhead, and a mother duck and her ducklings paddled across the lake. I saw frogs and turtles, intricate spiderwebs spun along the dock ladder, and curious fish swimming under lily pads. Life was happening all around me. As I sat witnessing the magnificence of all these little creatures, I knew that I was home.

After I bought the property, I decided to take up gardening. My neighbor Beth is an exceptional gardener. I had admired Beth's yard since the day I moved in. Her flowers were always blooming and rich with color. Whenever I saw her outside in her overalls and gardening gloves, I wanted to join in on the fun. She would offer me clippings and seeds from her flowers, but I never took her up on those offerings. Then one day I was lying in my bed in the city, pining over a breakup, when I had a thought: *I need to get out of here.* I grabbed my keys, hopped into Babe, and drove upstate. When I arrived, I texted Beth to ask if she had any flowers I could propagate. Within a few hours, she arrived at my place, pulling a red wagon full of peonies, irises, black-eyed Susans, astilbe, columbines, and roses.

"You think I can keep all these alive?" I asked.

"Only time will tell. Let's put them in the ground and see what takes," she said, beaming ear to ear.

"What do I do first?" I asked.

"First, you gotta have an intention for why you are gardening and what your garden will represent. This will help keep you invested." She proceeded to tell me her story, of how gardening played a role in her healing as a cancer survivor. "We had this hill in our backyard that my husband and I were always talking about cleaning up, but never did. Instead, we would complain about the overgrown weeds, dead bushes, and trees. When I found out I had cancer, depression set in fast. I started chemo, my hair fell out, and suddenly everything felt out of my control. My husband was incredibly supportive and kind, but his compassion only made me feel worse. One day I yelled at him for being so nice all of the time. He did not deserve my anger.

"From that moment on, I decided whenever I got mad I was going to take it out on that hill. When I was upset, we would go outside and pull weeds and rake, and I would yell at the weeds with their deep roots and curse at the dry soil and the rocks we dug up. Rain or shine, I would be out there working on that hill until I had nothing more to say.

"By the time we finished clearing the backyard, I was in remission. The whole time I was fighting cancer I wanted to believe I was going to win, but in the back of my mind I was prepared to die. I lived in fear that the doctor was going to tell me he made a mistake or the cancer had returned. But he never did.

"One day, my father brought me a container of peonies, and I planted them in the hill. I hadn't thought of gardening before, but from that day on, I planted flowers of gratitude for my healing. As I nurtured them and watched them grow, I found joy that melted away any fears. Gardening with intention is a powerful tool. What is it that you want to grow, Faith?"

I thought for a while, and I was embarrassed to admit that what I wanted was love. "Everybody around this lake has been married for decades. So I think a lot about committed partnership when I'm up here," I told her.

"Then this will be your love garden. From now on, you will think of the love that you want to sow and the love you want to reap. Tonight, make a list of the kind of man you want to meet and think of his character when you are gardening."

I was not quite as optimistic as Beth, but I had nothing to lose. For the rest of the weekend, I listened to Aretha Franklin sing love songs as I planted all the flowers. Then I began collecting rocks around the property to build a wall around the flower bed. Between the stones, I planted vinca, rosemary, and lavender. Neighbors offered stones from their homes, and I stayed outside working until my fingers were stiff.

I quickly learned that when you are a novice, gardening is a hobby you cannot take too seriously. There is a bit of mystery as to whether what you plant will grow, but that is part of why you keep at it. Of course, you want everything to live, though that doesn't always happen. Sometimes plants get diseased or are crowded out by an aggressive contender. There are times you think something is dead, only to realize it's very much alive. Finally, your rose bush blossoms, only to be eaten by insects. The work is messy, strenuous, and unpredictable, but that is the price you pay for fresh flowers.

Then there is the matter of having patience, as things take time to grow. This waiting period is not passive. It's filled with action, because every season requires some form of maintenance. A gardener has to water the seeds, pull the weeds, rake the leaves, lay down mulch, fertilize the soil, and turn the compost. When you commit to gardening, you commit to the labor and the journey. Gardening is an act of faith. You water seeds you cannot see, trusting something will germinate. Right when you're ready to give up, a leaf sprouts.

As with my garden, I encourage my clients to have an intention for their decluttering and organizing journey. As we approach the work holistically, I hope that organization is more than putting things in order. I hope we learn how to live a more meaningful life. Because when all is said and done, after we've closed the front door and there is no one around for whom to perform, we have to be able to find comfort and safety in the space we have created.

My goal is *not* to teach you how to have an insanely organized home with closets too precious to touch. My goal *is* to teach you how to be organized without the pressure of being perfect. Being organized does not mean being flawless. I'm organized, I'm not obsessive, I toss my clothes into a chest at the foot of my bed. I keep my underwear unfolded in a basket. I misplace my keys and often can't find my phone. I have a tiny linen closet with one shelf for linens, one for towels, and one for toiletries, which I toss in a box. Nothing is perfectly arranged, nothing is labeled, but it's all easy for me to find. There's no need to be meticulous. In short, you don't need a Pinterest-worthy pantry to be organized.

* * *

IMAGINE YOURSELF tossing your expectations out the window. Any fairy-tale ending that came to mind when you picked up this book, let it go. There is nothing to be perfected. Rather than thinking of housekeeping, organizing, and decluttering as the answer to your problems, think of this work as a way of being. Decluttering and organizing is an ongoing journey. You don't have to spring into action. You don't have to nail it. You don't even have to do it. If you decide to try, approach it as a practice. Here is my mantra: *Permission to try. Permission to fail. Permission to succeed.*

As long as you have a clear intention, you will keep showing up. Even when you feel like you have not made a dent, let your faith carry you through. My mission is to encourage you to believe in yourself, to act on your potential, to transform and create what you most desire. *To let your self grow.* Growing often means letting go and trusting there is more to you than your past or your possessions. Believe me, I did not learn this overnight. It took many iterations of "home" before I finally created one that felt truly my own. Through every move, I discovered a valuable truth: It's hard to feel at home if you do not feel at home in yourself.

Intention alone, however, isn't enough. At some point, reflection must meet reality. You have to get your hands on stuff. Bag it up. Take it out. Schedule the hauler. Make the decision. Donate the things. A dream without action is incomplete. Soul Work prepares the ground, but decluttering is what makes it fertile. Eventually, you'll have to move from understanding *why* to practicing *how*. That's when you truly begin the work of organizing.

REFLECTIVE QUESTIONS

As you embark on your organizing journey, use these questions to crystallize your intentions:

- What is my purpose for getting organized?
- What do I want to achieve through this process?
- How do I want to grow?
- What are my organizing expectations?
- Am I willing to release these expectations and embrace what comes naturally?

CHAPTER 8
LIFE TRANSITIONS

WE'VE DONE THE SOUL WORK: sifted through stories, recounted our pasts, confronted old beliefs, and clarified what truly matters most. Now we move into action. Sometimes action comes wrapped in change we didn't choose. Transitions, loss, and letting go of the life we once knew require us to shed things—not just physically but also emotionally. Decluttering is a response to change as well as a ritual that helps us move through it.

The early 1900s folklorist Arnold van Gennep studied the human experience of transition—those moments when we leave behind one version of ourselves and we step into another. Across cultures and classes, he found that life changes—marriage, parenthood, relocation, or loss—all follow the same three-step process. He called this process the "Rites of Passage." Each rite is pivotal to a person's transition from one state of being to another. Each rite may vary in intensity, but the order is always the same.

First is the *rite of separation*. This is the point at which the individual separates from their previous identity. Second is the *rite of transition*. The individual is no longer who they were but has yet to arrive at who they will be. This middle phase is crucial because the discomfort of displacement caused by being in limbo is what prepares a person for their new position. Last is the *rite of incorporation*, which is the moment the individual is established in their new identity or position, and is reincorporated back into society.

The act of decluttering is often triggered by a life transition; it puts an end to one phase and ushers in the next. If treated as such, this act of letting go has the potential to carry us more clearly into the next significant phase of our lives. Throughout this process, our character is put to the test, our identity is redefined, and life has new meaning. A graduation, a divorce, moving to a new home, losing a loved one, or making a career change are rites of passage that lead us to reevaluate our relationship to our surroundings. Accepting the inevitability of these moments will help ease us into each new phase of life.

As we move through the poignant seasons that make our lives unique, it's what we release that truly defines us.

* * *

AT THE START OF SPRING, Bliss's mother called me to help declutter her daughter's bedroom. Fourteen-year-old Bliss was in her last year of middle school. Over the years, she had developed a sincere attachment to her artwork and homework from the past. Her mother wanted Bliss to declutter, to make space for her high-school experiences ahead. When I walked into Bliss's bedroom, she was sitting by the window. Her mother introduced us, then excused herself to give us privacy.

Meeting with clients individually is my preferred method. I have found that people are more engaged in the process, and more honest, when we are one-on-one. If a parent, spouse, or roommate is nearby, some sarcasm, dismissiveness, and self-deprecation can take center stage and defeat the goal. When declutter sessions are more private, the person can speak freely, without fear or judgment.

Bliss had a somber disposition. She was soft-spoken and she moved with an air of fragility. I thought of myself as a teenager, clearing out my bedroom at the Erwins' house, and I felt compassion for her.

"Where would you like to begin?" I asked.

"Probably under my bed," she said.

She pulled out clear plastic containers of artwork and elementary-school work. As we studied the papers, we marveled at how her handwriting had changed over the years.

"What are you feeling?" I asked.

"I'm sad," Bliss whispered.

"Why?" I asked.

"I don't know. These papers remind me of a sweet time. I was so innocent back then. Things were simple." Her eyes began to well up with tears.

"My grandparents are already talking about college. Everything is about getting the right teachers and the best grades. Getting accepted into high school was stressful enough. I miss being younger," she said. Bliss traced the crayon strokes of an old drawing, her fingers lingering on the paper as if touching it would bring her earlier childhood back. "Things were easier then," she said softly, clutching the coloring book like a life raft. I explained that there would be challenges ahead as she took the steps toward young adulthood, that what she feared was lost was still within her, waiting to be summoned. She could still color, run, and play in the park. She could still do arts and crafts and wonder and explore. Her joy had become unreachable when she thought it was limited to her younger years.

"What if we could acknowledge those feelings, rather than letting them trap you in the past?" I suggested. "Let's put words to what these papers hold for you." I asked permission to pick up the papers. Then, with her assistance, we sorted them on the floor. I asked her to tag each pile with a word that encapsulated the emotion she felt when she looked at it. (I call this technique "emotional tagging.") I explained it is not how you felt about an object in the past but how it makes you feel now. We stuck a Post-it note on each pile of papers. She tagged them with emotions like "sadness," "anger," "missing a friend."

"I have a suggestion, let's pull out your favorite pieces from each pile. Then we are going to release everything that represents a negative emotion. Even if something represents a time in your life that was amazing, if you don't feel that way when you look at it now, let it go. When you do this, you will honor both your past and your present." I then pulled out the trash can from under her desk. "Whatever you let go of, remember that it's not the moment you loved that we are getting rid of but, rather, the longing that has gotten in the way."

We worked for the next three hours. We moved on from the papers that had been under her bed to the boxes that were on her bookshelf, investigating and emotionally tagging each one. By the end, when her mother returned, we had consolidated what was left into one box, placed on the bottom shelf of her bookcase. Everything in it represented cherished moments of Bliss's life's journey, and we had created space for her faith in the future.

* * *

EMOTIONAL TAGGING grants us the permission to let go of whatever we have projected onto an object. Labeling something the way it makes us feel helps us recognize what exactly we are holding on to. Letting go is a sacred affair that offers agency over our lives as we move through each rite of passage. I use emotional tagging to help light the way for others on the path to newness. The decluttering then grounds the participants and positions them to accept and welcome their future. I have found this to be true numerous times, whether it's the decluttering that's done after losing a spouse or parent, or it's someone like Bliss who is making space for new memories. When we take the time to listen, process our emotions, and accept the reality of a life change, we become active participants in our evolution. Our life transitions are no longer happening to us. They are happening with us. Making space for the unknown is an acceptance and affirmation that change is coming. Letting go of our possessions carves a path for something new to enter our lives.

Let's get specific about why we declutter. What do you suppose is the connection between the excess in our homes and the life transitions that push us to let go? Perhaps you walk into your bedroom, and suddenly it feels off. The air is stale. Piles of papers and scattered belongings line the baseboards. The chair in the corner, once inviting, is covered in unfolded laundry. The clothes in your closet don't match the person you are. This feeling of being a stranger in your own room doesn't come out of nowhere. It's a signal. It signals that a shift has already begun within you, and your home is reflecting the need for change. When we pay attention to these cues, we can move toward transformation with intention, rather than with resistance.

Make the editing of your space a ceremony, a ritual you partake in. This ceremony could be done quarterly, annually, or when you reach particular milestones in your life. Choose to make this Soul Work and decluttering part of your life course.

As I did with Bliss, take a stack of Post-its and walk around a space where you feel uncomfortable. Write down one word to describe the emotion you feel about each item in the room. Remember that this exercise is not about what you used to feel, or what you hope to feel. It is about what you feel *right now*. Write whatever comes to mind—these words will become emotional snapshots of your personal possessions.

To understand what you are attached to, step back and see what emotions surround you. This will help you realize what you are releasing. Suddenly, you will not be letting go of that journal you have had since you were twenty. Instead, you'll be letting go of the anxiety you felt during that period in your life. Or, as in Bliss's case, you will be releasing what once represented the best time of your life, creating space for something even better.

* * *

HARRY AND JOANNA were customers at the restaurant where I worked many years ago. Both were professors, and their home reflected their passion for learning. Their bookcases were full, and the side tables were stacked with magazines and newspapers. I often borrowed books from them and, after turning the last page, would share my thoughts with the couple. On weekends, we'd drive out to Connecticut to clear the estate of Harry's godmother. Joanna took care of everything—hiring the movers, liquidators, and contractors—while Harry and I followed her instructions. Afterward, we'd go out to dinner and recap the day. Harry was a collector of all sorts, and when they inherited the estate, their apartment quickly filled with more books, art, and trinkets from his travels. When their home clutter became overwhelming, Joanna hired me to help sort and stash their surplus out of view.

"I remember when he first let me into his apartment before we got married. I cried," she admitted as we double-stacked the books on the shelves. Joanna claimed she wasn't as attached to their things as Harry was, although over the years she had become just as sentimental.

As my organizing business grew, I stopped working for them

professionally, yet our relationship had evolved into a close friendship. They gave me life advice as I navigated my broken engagement, the move to my studio, and the pressures of running a business. When I first started working for them, Joanna told me she had Parkinson's disease. Her symptoms were barely detectable at that point. "I'm going to fight this, Faith," she used to say as we organized her pill boxes. Her optimism fluctuated depending on the day. But in a few years, her tremors increased. Harry took over the household tasks, did the cooking, and kept Joanna socially and physically active. During the pandemic, I stopped visiting them, and we switched to virtual dinner dates. They put their housekeeper on hold, and Harry struggled to keep up with the apartment while caring for Joanna.

"We've got to get this place together. I love my husband, but there's too much stuff in here," she'd say, as Harry bounced across the computer screen, carrying a bag of groceries. Then the calls slowed down. I reached out for updates on Joanna's health, only to learn that Harry had cancer. It was aggressive, but they stayed optimistic. Joanna put all her energy into his care, just as he had for her. She changed their diet, made his juices, attended every chemo appointment. Despite his hair loss, surgery scars, and rounds of chemo, Harry was still folding the laundry, telling stories, and laughing with me over the phone. I wanted to believe we'd be celebrating his healing in a year, but then the doctors gave him two weeks to live.

I called Joanna. "How can I help?"

"We need to turn his home office into a room for the caregiver. Can you come tonight?"

When I arrived, his family was there—his mother, sister, brother, nieces, and nephews, all grouped around him. I slipped into the back room and began sorting the trash and moving papers into boxes to create space for the aide. Every time I tried to take a bag out, Harry would stop me at the door. "What's in the bag?" he'd ask. I'd step forward, open it, and show him.

Before I left that day, I asked if I could borrow a couple of books that looked interesting. He nodded yes. Because of the pandemic, I couldn't give him a hug or hold his hand. My mask robbed us of sharing our last smile. Harry died two days later.

After the funeral, Joanna hired me to clear his faculty office, located near the university. The rent was expensive and the lease was nearly up. I wanted to help, but the thought of going through his belongings made me sick to my stomach. The day I finally mustered the courage to go, I could feel his presence in the room. Joanna had given me the key, and I stood there alone, surrounded by things that embodied Harry's passion for learning and teaching.

"I know you don't want me getting rid of anything, Harry," I murmured. "But the cost of this office is unnecessary if you're not here."

The family had already taken what they wanted, but there were still shelves of books left. "No one wants the books or the bookcase," my assistant said. "Should we call a junk removal service or donate them?"

"Did you check with Joanna?" I asked.

"She says they already have two storage units full of books, plus the ones at the house."

"I'll take the bookcase," I said.

"And the books?"

I hesitated. "Yes. I'll take those, too."

The next day, I hauled thirty-eight boxes of books from Harry's office to my apartment. They sat in the center of the room, looming.

I struggled to let them go. I thought about Harry's legacy, the time he spent curating this collection. *What would he think if I gave them away?* For days, I stepped around the boxes, unwilling to part with them. Even after moving some furniture to accommodate the boxes, I couldn't shake the weight of their presence. Finally, I set a deadline: two weeks. If I couldn't find a home for the books by then, I'd toss the textbooks and donate the rest.

I emailed the university where Harry had worked, contacted the library, and reached out to a few organizations connected with his research. No one wanted the books. A week passed. Then I stumbled across a community book swap that agreed to take them all. The day the books left my apartment, I cried. My space was back. Sadly, my friend was still gone.

* * *

LOSING A LOVED ONE is an experience that's completely out of your control. Keeping everything of theirs is tempting, like my instinct to keep Harry's books, yet the things we're holding on to can't stand in for the person we've lost. As our own mortality comes into view, those emotions can be difficult to face, but when we do, we make space for healing. Every emotion we come up against throughout the seasons of loss invites us to love ourselves more.

So, take a breath—maybe a few—and let those breaths commemorate a new chapter in your life. The more you put into order emotionally and mentally, the more rewarding your homemaking will be. This practice will become easier with time.

REFLECTIVE QUESTIONS

As you contemplate a loss, ask yourself:

- What do I want to make peace with in my life?

- What material possessions represent the moments in my life I want to heal?
- What will letting go of these possessions mean to me?
- How might the absence of these things change the atmosphere of my home?

CHAPTER 9

THE ART OF LETTING GO

When a family hired Organize With Faith to clear out their mother's estate, we were told to separate what was essential from what was trash, and from there, to provide a report with pictures. As we sorted the piles for the liquidators and appraisers to evaluate, we found that most things weren't worth much. Once-prized possessions—crystal vases, landscape oil paintings, fur coats—had depreciated as people's tastes changed. The family may have gotten an offer for the Persian rug, but the amount would barely cover a single day's labor. The pieces of antique furniture they assumed were worth a fortune turned out to be replicas. In truth, I have yet to meet a person who has gotten rich from clearing out an estate.

We sorted every coat, cabinet, and dresser drawer. We took out countless contractor bags of trash, and scheduled junk removal and shredding services to deal with the papers that represented an entire life. We shipped to the family members what they had wanted, then hired cleaners, did the walk-through with the super, and turned in the key. By the time we were done, there was only an outline of what used to be there—empty walls and hardwood floors.

The project took a week and a half. That was ten days to empty an apartment someone had lived in for thirty-five years. The emotional toll was palpable, from the initial shock of the task at hand to the bittersweet feeling of leaving behind a space that once held life. We rarely think about our mortality when we accumulate our belongings.

In our work, if things aren't sold, they're donated. If they can't be given away, they're junked. Imagine if someone had to go through everything you own right now. Would it seem to them like a collection of meaningful, intentional objects? Or, would it feel like a burden? Would your belongings reflect the history you want to tell? Or, would it be piles of unfinished projects, stacks of unopened mail, and items you kept out of guilt?

On any given day in my work as a professional organizer, I could pull up to a beach house in the Hamptons, dressed in my best, or enter a court-ordered project in a hazmat suit. Regardless of the location or income bracket, the work is the same. I help people reorganize their lives by unpacking their complicated relationships with their belongings. I'd be lying if I said that clearing away clutter is easy. I struggled to get rid of Harry's textbooks, and he wasn't even my family.

I understand that things matter. They are a record of our existence. In many ways, possessions are so alluring because they are so dependable. They bring us back to a part of ourselves we used to be. They hold memories of different times and different places. In the case of inheritance, bequeathed objects remind us of those we love. When does holding on to those things shift from meaningful to overwhelming? The line between cherishing and accumulating isn't always clear. If we're not mindful, we risk being consumed by what we once treasured.

Despite our frustrations and discomfort, we still struggle to understand that the things that spark joy can also be what stand in our way. If you love every object or outfit in your home, but feel weighed down and drained when you step into a room, something is not adding up.

We can't love it all. Even when we try to convince ourselves that we can, we feel the opposite when we're surrounded by it all. We're not better off with all those things. We're overwhelmed. We hold on to things out of love, memory, obligation, or guilt. We tell ourselves we should keep them because they were expensive, or they were given to us as gifts, or we *might* need them someday.

The price we pay for an object isn't when we buy it, it's when we bring it home. Every item we keep should serve us. If not, then it becomes a weight that we carry. Joy is freedom. The more belongings we have, the less freedom we have. Managing stuff takes up our time, money, energy, and attention, time we could be giving to ourselves and to our loved ones.

* * *

NAOMI'S SISTER reached out to me for help. She described Naomi as a passionate individual who often found herself overwhelmed by unfinished projects. When I arrived, it was evident her home was filled not just with unfinished projects but also with the weight of unmade decisions.

When we tackled her guest room closet, it was stacked to the ceiling with rows of acrylic containers. They were filled with craft supplies, emergency kits, unopened gifts, and tools for hobbies she never had time to pursue. At one point, she planned to start a garden and had purchased seeds for all kinds of flowers, but never got around to planting them. She took up knitting and bought enough yarn to make sweaters, scarves, and socks, but she never found the time to knit. Her passions were real, but the supplies consistently outpaced the time she had to use them.

I handed her a box I'd found in the closet, wrapped in gold paper and tied with a ribbon. "Who is Jessica?" she asked, turning over the gift tag. "I don't even know who this is. I must have bought this gift years ago." That moment was like a mirror reflecting years of delayed plans. The things Naomi had gathered for what she wanted to do were now reminders of what never happened.

We made our way through the craft supplies, and Naomi sighed, sinking onto the sofa. "This is hard." She pulled out a set of stencils, flipping through them like a deck of cards. She ran her fingers over the designs. "I stenciled the nursery walls when we were getting the room ready, but that was a long time ago. I always thought I would stencil the dining table chairs. But they can go," she said, setting the stencils aside.

As consumers, we all run into this habit—buying items that represent the life we want to live but can't always make time for. The hardest part of this isn't letting go of the things themselves. It's making peace with the reality of not getting to live the life we imagined when we bought them. I asked Naomi what legacy she wanted to leave her daughter. Were these unfinished projects truly what mattered? Or, was there something more meaningful she wanted to pass on? At the heart of it, decluttering isn't simply about getting rid of stuff. It's about what we leave behind.

At the end of the day, Naomi and I made peace with the yarn she never used, the seeds she never planted, and the gifts she never gave. She came to the realization that the clutter of unrealized hobbies and unfinished tasks was not the legacy she wanted to leave for her daughter. Nor was it something she wanted to live with. We accepted the fact that some doors in life quietly close, but that doesn't mean another door doesn't open. We released everything that was no longer relevant. In doing so, Naomi realized that the actual loss was not the things we gave away but, rather, the space those things had taken up in her home and the pressure of unfinished passions.

* * *

UNDERSTANDING WHY we hold on to things is one part of the work. Letting go is the other part. If you find yourself unmotivated or exhausted at the thought of pulling everything out, take that as a sign. If the act of sorting through your belongings drains you, what makes you think maintaining those belongings isn't doing the same? Every item you own demands energy. If it's too much to face now, it's too much to carry forward.

When we clear space, we should be intentional about what fills it next. This keeps us engaged with the present and with our life's potential. So, only keep what you can care for. If something is worth keeping, it should be worth the effort to maintain, actively engage with, store, and appreciate. The true work of making a home is in reclaiming your time and curating your legacy.

Before moving on to organizing, be honest about what you have and why you have it. Ask yourself:

- If I moved tomorrow, what would I take with me?
- If I passed away, would the things I've held on to offer comfort or create stress for those I love?
- What would I genuinely miss if my things were destroyed in a natural disaster?

Letting go is an act of intentionally shaping our environment to reflect the people we are today. Instead of dreading this act, we can view it as a way to lighten our mental and emotional loads. The people we love may not remember us for the possessions we hold on to. They will remember how we made them feel, the time we spent with them, the love we shared.

If you don't know where to begin, try this: Close your eyes and mentally walk through your home. Mentally open every drawer, cabinet, and closet. Can you see everything clearly? If a space feels fuzzy, that means energy is stuck there. It's a place you don't often go. That place is your starting point.

The best way to declutter is to be thorough and to sort intentionally, rather than rushing through. Sorting in preparation for decluttering will reveal the full scale of what you own. I've had some clients who refuse to sort thoroughly. People are so rushed to finish the job that they neglect to do it *thoroughly*. The result? There's a back room or closet still filled with items that have no real home or purpose. The difficulty often lies in taking the time to sift through the minutiae and think critically if even the smallest things are worth keeping. Deciding what stays and what goes doesn't have to feel chaotic. The more structured your approach, the easier it becomes.

Here are some decluttering basics:

1. **Choose a space or category to work on.** Select a drawer, a closet, a room, books, papers, etc., to sort. When you choose an area or subject, stay with it. If you're focused on papers, collect all the papers throughout the house so you can go through them all at once. Don't reroute to shopping for containers or decluttering the clothes. Stick with whatever you start with. If you bounce between categories, you'll never see progress.

2. **Set a time to declutter.** Start with thirty minutes, take a break, then return to it. Work on your ability to be fully present, easing your way up from thirty minutes to an hour,

to four hours of dedicated decluttering time. (Note: Each decluttering session should include the time to transport your donations.)

3. **Sort quickly—don't overthink it.** This is not the time to make decisions about whether you should keep things, or where they should go. This is the prep work for decluttering, so pull everything out, empty every container, and put like item with like item. Be specific. This will help you stay focused, and when it comes time to edit, you'll have context.

4. **Let go without guilt.** Think about what you want and what you hope to create with this new space. If you run into unexpected emotions, go back to your Soul Work. Try the emotional tagging exercise. When it's time to let go, assess whether the objects measure up to who you are, what you believe, how you choose to live, and what you value. Instead of asking how much did the item cost or what if you might need it someday, ask, *Does this add value to my life?* or, *How has this been helpful to me?* Remember, things are only as valuable as you make them.

   When it's time to let go, separate the memorabilia and be selective about what you keep. How much do you truly need to commemorate a specific moment in your life? In most cases, a select piece or two will ground you in a cherished memory. If items represent a significant memory, treat them that way—showcase your beloved possessions, don't shove them into the back of a closet.

5. **Acknowledge the fear, then act anyway.** It's normal to feel resistance when letting go. If you're dealing with something that's inherited, remember that the things are not them. More important, what you keep is not contingent on how you have loved.

6. **Deep-clean.** Wipe down the shelves, vacuum the floors, and spruce up the area before returning remaining items. A clean space makes for a proper reset and might inspire you to declutter further.

7. **Repeat.** Letting go is a habit you build, not a onetime event. Decluttering isn't something you finish. Make it a part of your lifestyle. Each time you let go, you improve your ability to make space for what truly matters and you hone your decision-making skills.

A home filled with meaning is far more valuable than one filled with things. Decluttering gets hard when emotions rise to the surface. You may feel resistance, frustration, and exhaustion. You may start and stop, finding yourself stuck in decision fatigue. The key is persistence.

I am good at clearing clutter. That's not because it's easy or I am exceptionally talented. I am good at it because experience has taught me that if I keep showing up and working toward the goal, I will eventually complete the task. There are days when I don't feel like doing the work. On those days, I do a little at a time. I start small, and I trust that the next day, I'll tackle something more. My *commitment to the process* is what makes every project a success.

Persistence keeps us going. When the task seems overwhelming (and decluttering will at times feel incredibly overwhelming), we stay the course. It will take time, yes. Patience is a variable that most people want to ignore, yet it's integral to the decluttering and organizing process.

Decluttering is not magic. We are not robots who tidy up a mess in a millisecond. We are human beings working through decades of accumulated clutter. Day 1 may seem impossible, day 3 may feel like you are drowning in chaos, but by day 5 or 6, the space begins to open up and there is light at the end of the tunnel. The satisfaction of making progress and of finishing what you set out to do is indescribable. Every action slowly chips away at that which at first seemed impenetrable. Letting go can be hard, but that doesn't mean it's impossible.

* * *

ORGANIZING IS OFTEN mistaken for making things look pretty. Professional organizers are seen folding shirts neatly, lining up objects on shelves, and tucking everything into matching baskets. Our things are excellent placeholders, but they can't replace the joy we get from fulfilling our lives, connecting with those we love, and pursuing our dreams. The goal is not to strip our homes bare. It's to create space for what matters most.

I've seen clients keep entire wardrobes from a life they no longer lead—clothes for jobs they left, sizes they no longer wear, aspirations they've outgrown. They say, "I'll wear this again someday." But someday never comes. When they go to get dressed and look in their closet full of clothes, they'll say, "I have nothing to wear." Because they don't—not anything that represents who they are today.

For others, it's not about clothing. It's about relationships. People hold on to furniture they hate simply because it belonged to a relative. They're not holding on to the upright piano they don't know how to play, or have no room for. They're holding on to the love and the memories the piano represents, trying to fill a sense of loss. Here's the truth: Keeping the object won't bring the person back. That person's impact and presence live in *you*, not in the furniture collecting dust in the corner.

Then there's the fear—the *What if I need this later?* mentality. I've worked with people who hold on to broken appliances, outdated electronics, and boxes of items they haven't touched in years. They tell themselves they might fix it, use it, or need part of it. The reality is that by clinging to the past or preparing for every possible future, they are sacrificing the present. Keep what you can care for and use. Keep select items that have meaning. Be clear in your intention regarding your legacy so there's no question about what you're leaving behind and why.

I'm not here to tell you that letting go will make you happier. I'm here to remind you that life is meant to be lived. Not in the past, but in the present. The things we let go of aren't losses—they're choices. They are choices to make things easier on ourselves and our loved ones. They are choices to create the space to move forward. To make room for new memories, new experiences, new priorities, and new possibilities.

On page 193, you'll find the Soul Work Workbook. This is the same workbook I give to clients during the earliest stages of our journey together. Setting aside the time to reflect on your personal history, your attachments to your belongings, and your ideas of home will begin to loosen your grip on things. The point of this process isn't to force change. It's to create the space for you to reflect and to welcome what's new. When you find yourself stuck, turn to the workbook. Use its reflective questions to explore your past and your present, and help to cultivate a more meaningful decluttering and organizing practice.

REFLECTIVE QUESTIONS

- What am I holding on to that no longer serves me?
- If someone had to go through my belongings today, what would they see?
- Am I prioritizing things over experiences? Am I prioritizing possessions over people?
- If I free up space, how will I feel about that empty space?
- How can I make the process of decluttering and organizing a practice, not a onetime event?

* * *

IN PART TWO: HOME WORK, we explore the strategies, components, and principles of organizing. As you begin, remember this: Before you start organizing, you must practice letting go. When you do, you don't just clear space in your home—you clear space in your heart and mind.

PART TWO

HOME WORK

CHAPTER 10

INTERNAL HOUSEKEEPING

EVERY DAY, our bodies consume, sort, and release. Through breath, sweat, waste, or tears, we rid ourselves of what we no longer need. Gradual changes in our bodies reveal our growth. As children, we may fall and bleed, but eventually we heal. It's amazing how even the scars of our past pains soften with time. The mind may loop our best and worst memories, but the body remains present. It does not hold on to an extinct version of itself to prove its existence. Our looks may change, yet we are still wholly *us*.

Beneath the surface, a network of nerves, cells, and organs carries out a divine act of housekeeping. This organized system continuously measures and directs what enters it—filtering out toxins, absorbing nutrients, and protecting what matters. These acts of self-care are nonnegotiable. If consumption stops, so does life. If elimination halts, the system collapses. Sorting and elimination are so intrinsically tied to our existence that it's automatic. We don't manage our digestion, circulation, or immune responses. They just happen. When they are in tune with our bodies, they operate in an astonishing order. When they are out of tune, stress wreaks havoc on a system that's meant to keep us healthy and strong.

The body is also a vessel for the spirit, allowing us to act out dreams or share messages of love with others. In good health, the body thrives, maintaining an environment in which the soul can flourish. So, let your home be for the body what the body is for the soul. Your home should function with the same internal clarity as your body, consuming what nourishes, releasing what burdens, and maintaining systems that support vitality. To consume is essential and to filter and release is crucial to our well-being. We block our pathways when we forsake the necessary habits of assessing, sorting, directing, and releasing what enters our home.

* * *

WE ALL LIKE TO THINK we have a handle on things, that we know what we have, why we have it, and where it is. This sense of awareness is often false, however. The moment we start pulling everything out, unpacking drawers and emptying bins, we realize exactly how much we don't know. The illusion of control ceases as we confront the sheer volume of our consumption.

The first step to restoring order is admitting we've lost track. If your home feels cramped, assess your back stock, the surplus items that are often stashed away, like toiletries, paper towels, or pantry goods. Compare it to the value of your square footage. What does this square footage mean emotionally, physically, and monetarily? Are the things occupying this space worth the cost of that space? Back stock is for our economic benefit and convenience, but it should never exist at the expense of our contentment. During Covid, we saw this full force. Some people still have toilet paper from 2020 stacked in their garage. We "subscribe and save," often underestimating how long it takes to use the items we have purchased in bulk. Spend some time to observe the life cycle of your purchases. Track how long it takes to finish that toothpaste, shampoo, or soap. In the end, having excess creates congestion. Too much of anything causes discomfort.

Many of us have entered a vicious cycle of repeat buying before we run out of certain products. Overconsumption often stems from an internal anxiety or mindset of lack. That is, having more than enough gives us a sense of security in an uncertain world. If anxiety arises at the thought of running out of an item that is readily available on the internet or in local stores, then investigate what that feeling stems from. This will help you determine if the acquisition of back stock is attached to an emotional insecurity.

Like the body, our homes carry the weight of our decisions. Overconsumption overloads the home and keeps it from functioning properly. Our home is not meant to be perfect. It is meant to be used, cleansed, and cared for.

* * *

I CANNOT STRESS THIS ENOUGH: Home organizing is domestic labor. Organizing and cleaning are connected. No component of homemaking stands alone. If one aspect is missing—whether it be Soul Work, decluttering, organizing, or cleaning—the rest falters. Without designated places for our belongings, we either clean around them or stop cleaning altogether. Even hired help can only do so much—they wipe surfaces, but they can't perform a true deep cleaning if clutter is in the way.

When we do our own cleaning, it brings us in direct contact with our possessions, prompting us to regularly reconsider whether those items genuinely belong in our lives. Ask yourself: Is this worth cleaning and regularly maintaining? We tend to become less likely to overconsume when our organizing routines involve removing items to deep-clean, evaluating their necessity, then intentionally placing them back. It is then that we may find that a lot of things are not worth the time. Cleaning invites us to reconsider what deserves space and attention in our homes.

When we housekeep, we reconnect to our space. Cleanliness brings forth clarity. Start your organizing journey by cleaning a single area. Remove everything from a drawer, cabinet, or surface. Wipe it down, sort the items, and then put them back. This task alone will inspire you to declutter and reorganize. Most people come to realize they don't want to clutter a clean space.

Even those who hire housecleaners benefit from participating in this process. Many people tidy up before the cleaner arrives, so as to appear less messy or to make it easier for the cleaner to do the work. That impulse says something about us. While cleaning, we also gather information—for instance, how we want things done, what areas we're struggling with, what we're running out of have too much of. Or, we uncover the leak behind the faucet. We also discover the potential organizing systems we can create. In fact, the more we do, the more we know.

Housekeeping grounds us in ownership. If we avoid it, we become disconnected from our spaces and our habits. That disconnect shows up in overconsumption or indifference to our surroundings. However, cleaning reconnects us. It reminds us of what we have and what we need to do.

Start by removing trash that's already meant to go: empty bottles, take-out containers, junk mail, torn packaging, and boxes from your last online order. Gather cans of old paint and other hazardous household waste, and take that to a community collection event or a hazardous waste facility. Recycle any ripped or stained linens, textiles, and clothes that can't be donated. Taking out the trash regularly, whether weekly or several times a week, is one of the easiest ways to stay ahead of the clutter.

The truth is that traces of consumption linger in every home. Similar to how the body automatically releases what it doesn't need, homes need that same cleansing rhythm. Remove what's expired, broken, unwanted, or obsolete. Repurpose what you can, only if you'll actually use it. If you're saving empty condiment jars, use them to store buttons, paperclips, stamps, cords, or tea. Or, use them to pack up snacks, decant dried beans, or hold cotton swabs or makeup brushes.

We often have ideas we prepare for but never execute. Now is the time to execute those ideas, or at least try. We may find that they are not worth the hassle. Don't waste your space on unrealized potential. Be specific about how you're reusing the items you're collecting, and be selective. If you like a particular container, save only that type of container. Once your needs are met, stop collecting them. The trick to organizing is to know and employ what you need, then release the rest.

When it comes to gadgets and cords, if it's not in use and you don't know what it belongs to, let it go. If everything is plugged in and working, then keep one spare cord but know that there is no use for spares of spares. Sometimes, people resist disposing of unrecognizable cords because they fear they will need them one day. If that is the case, figure out what the cord belongs to. If you are not interested in figuring that out, why keep it? Again, we're not talking about cords in use—these are cords that are taking up space in your drawers or bins, with no purpose. These are all low-hanging fruit, as they are objects rarely carrying emotional weight and so can easily be shed.

* * *

PAPERS ARE A BEAST, but you can tame them in two phases.

- **Phase 1:** Gather all your loose paper from every bag, drawer, and surface, including newsletters, receipts, flyers, dated announcements, tickets, notes, and mail. As the events pass, those papers become clutter. Toss what's expired or irrelevant. If there are dates that you want to remember, put them into your calendar. If mailers are invasive, call the companies and ask to be removed from their mailing lists. If you've already paid a bill and it's reflected on your credit card or bank statement, you generally don't need to keep the paper copy. Hold on to only the statements or bills that need your attention—anything unresolved, required for taxes, or a part of an ongoing issue. Papers take up space and mental energy.

- **Phase 2:** Sort through what's left, dividing it into categories before you begin to declutter or file the papers. Make stacks, as appropriate: medical, financial, utilities, taxes, work, personal notes, keepsakes. Then sort each stack by year, if need be. If you have full file cabinets or storage boxes, take out the files and add them to the categories as well. From there on, you declutter one category at a time. Start with the least daunting category so you can build momentum. Begin connecting the dots, recalling to-dos, revisiting responsibilities, filing current documents, and regaining control.

On to photos . . . I have spent hours sifting through old photographs with clients. Oftentimes they have no idea who the people are in the pictures. These stacks of photos can be packed with duplicates, or the smiling faces are cut off by the frame. Many will have been taken of random landscapes or a monkey at the zoo. As time passes, those photographs don't do the memories justice. Take time to go through them all, setting aside those without meaning. You'll be surprised at how many images you're willing to discard. Organize the ones you want to keep, and store them in boxes or albums if you're feeling inspired. You can also have your photos professionally digitized. Keeping them stored separately from your computer's hard drive makes them easier to revisit and share.

* * *

WE NEED TO *FEEL* the time and energy it takes to manage our possessions. That awareness slows the cycle of acquisition. The more we get into the habit of the small things, like handling our returns, getting on top of our papers, or recycling what we no longer need, the more aware we are of the cost of our consumption.

Likewise, the way we consume matters. Shop with intention. Make a list of what you need and what you are willing to replace. Try to use what you have. When you do shop, shop mindfully. How we monitor our input and output significantly affects each system we create. This consumption also includes containers, baskets, boxes, dividers, and anything else marketed to help you get "organized." Pause. If your grandparents didn't need them to be organized, neither do you.

Organizing is essentially bodywork. It requires physical movement, inner stillness, and our willingness to release. Turning within to follow our instincts releases the idea that any person's method or aesthetic is a rule. Everything we need to organize an environment that fosters our well-being exists within our internal landscape. If we focus on assessing our consumption, sorting, directing, and eliminating excess, then we will meet our goals.

The next three chapters consider the principles of foundational organizing and decluttering—Principle One: Awareness; Principle Two: Boundaries; and Principle Three: Adjustments. They are an alternative way to think about home organization. You can apply these principles to any method you want, or use them as the foundation for your next organizing project. The principles can sustain systems and become the glue that binds those systems together. They will deepen your practice and provide clarity as you organize a home in alignment with your values and well-being.

Remember, without clear principles, concepts fail, structures collapse, and all the hard work, money, and time is wasted. Let the following chapters shift your mindset, enrich your course of action, and empower your homemaking. If you commit to these principles, your homemaking practice will never be the same. You will be at the center—the architect and the inhabitant—building a shelter for your mind, body, and soul.

REFLECTIVE QUESTIONS

When you think about the connection between housekeeping and home organizing, ask yourself:

- How can I make organizing a part of my housekeeping routine?
- How do I feel about cleaning and how can I incorporate it into my organizing process?
- When was the last time I deep-cleaned my home? If I were to do it again, where would I start?

CHAPTER 11

PRINCIPLE ONE: AWARENESS

> Awareness: Knowing something; knowing something exists and is important; being interested in something
>
> —*Oxford English Dictionary*

IN PART ONE, I shared the story of my mama discovering a single crumb on the counter and immediately knowing someone had been in the house. If there was ever an anecdote to describe her, that would be it. She knew what she had, where it belonged, and what needed to be done—because she was *aware*.

As I've grown, I've come to admire her domestic eye and creative spirit. The ability to notice, feel, and sense when something is off is a talent to be honed. More than that, her sense of awareness influenced the way she organized our home. My mama isn't the type of woman who follows the rules. She trusts her instincts, and as a result, she makes spaces that are uniquely hers. From her, I learned that making a home is a practice of tending to your needs. Knowing yourself, and others, is essential to the work.

The key to getting organized is found in our ability to notice what is happening around us and within us. Awareness is the first step toward reclaiming your home.

* * *

TO BE AWARE is to be accountable. The information we gain from having self-awareness encourages us to improve, adapt, and change. To know our capacity and incapacities is to accept the responsibility of our choices.

Many of us choose to be selectively self-aware. We know what makes us tick in our platonic, romantic, or familial relationships. At work, we know what we need to do to meet our deadlines and responsibilities. We tell others about our childhood traumas and how they connect to the major themes in our lives. In public, we are often highly aware of what is happening around us, but once we get home and are faced with organizing our things, life becomes a mystery. It's as if the information we've gathered has nothing to do with the homes we create. As if our state of mind has no influence on how we perceive our spaces.

When we opt out of self-awareness, we dismiss our knowledge, agency, and authority. Self-awareness leads to spatial awareness. We can study the spatial awareness of others, but we must also learn how to harness our own. Our understanding of what we need and why we need it determines the outcome of our environment. To practice spatial awareness, we have to be able to look at a space objectively, without judgment or condemnation.

Walking through a space without an impulse to fix, justify, or defend what we see allows us to view the space more clearly. Observing with all our senses, accepting the contents in every drawer, closet, and room, is the beginning of growth. Developing spatial awareness is not about decluttering or getting organized. Spatial awareness is about observing the essence of a space and the materials that define the state of our homes.

When I'm working with a client, I arrive early to study the space. Although getting the place organized is my intention and job, I don't start organizing right away. I take pictures to review, often on the subway or before bed. Even when the images show a complete mess, they reveal a lot about the way someone lives. While assessing a space, I do not try to come up with a solution or prepare a to-do list. Wide-angle shots of the rooms give me a bird's-eye view, and more close-up photos of opened cabinets and drawers allow me to zoom in.

Finding organizing solutions is not one-size-fits-all. You have to understand the nuances of the space and the people who live there. You must be *present*. When the mind is free to observe, it will gather information and start to shuffle that information to make sense. As we begin to work here, you'll be surprised at the solutions that can arise as a result of simply assessing a space. If excess threatens your capacity to explore, make note of that, but don't let it define the home or trigger you to act impulsively.

Having unrealistic expectations, striving for perfection, and being rigid are not organizing skills. When things are styled without connection, placed without purpose, accepted without examination, and discarded without understanding, all to embody a prototype, this fosters regret. Domestic burnout ensues when we are misaligned. This misalignment happens when we deny the body its natural inclination to process the environment it inhabits.

The pressure to build systems without fault—and spaces that look untouched—is a social construct. When we develop a domestic experience built upon this construct, we are consistently defeated and disappointed as our expectations go unmet. Awareness is the key to organization. It's important to know why things are where they are, how they got there, and who they benefit. Understanding what we need and how we operate shapes the systems put into place.

There are four types of awareness to consider when making a home:

1. **Awareness of yourself:** This is of your needs, attachments, impulses, desires, and restrictions. Personal awareness highlights the mental and physical habits that contribute to the intricacies of your homemaking.

2. **Awareness of your belongings:** This is of your home's contents—their purpose and necessity. Through this awareness, you understand how these belongings connect and how often you engage, consume, and care for the items that define your space.

3. **Awareness of your space:** This is of the home as a whole—how the home feels and functions and what the home requires. Spatial awareness also means being aware of your influence on the atmosphere around you.

4. **Awareness of others:** This is of those with whom you share the space. What are their domestic strengths and weaknesses, their habits, needs, and goals for the space you share? How do you work as a team to make a harmonious home?

Awareness in any capacity is a practice to be developed. How many times have we set something down and forgotten where we put it? To avoid overworking, our brains memorize what we do most frequently, leading to blocks of time that are mentally unaccounted for. The hours blend, the days blur, and the panic of being unable to remember our actions is an obstacle stopping us from reuniting with what is lost. In these ordinary moments, we awaken to the importance of our attention.

Organizing is an undeniably attractive activity, as it frees us from confusion. If everything has its place, we have no need to wonder where to put something. If systems can prompt an activity, the activity becomes automatic. For instance, I swap my clothes every winter and spring. Whatever is not in season goes into two fabric boxes. I have also gotten into the habit of decluttering as I make this seasonal transition. My letting go of unwanted clothing is no longer based on my mood but on habit. In this way, I have created a consistent rhythm.

The same goes for my kitchen. If I cannot easily access the food in my fridge, there is a good chance something will spoil. I clear out and clean my refrigerator once a week as I make my grocery list. I also reorganize my refrigerator when I am putting my groceries away. Since I do this weekly, the process doesn't take long. I end up saving time and money because I know what I have. I do not sift through rotten or expired food, and I do not buy duplicates.

Having regular actions in place protects our energy and ensures our peace of mind. However, when we've lived in places for years and grown accustomed to how things have been, we often struggle to reinvent those places. Developing spatial awareness, especially in overly familiar places, is both a skill and a necessary component of organizing. Practice mindfulness, playfulness, and critical thinking to reorient you to your space.

MINDFULNESS

Through mindfulness, we free ourselves of the discouragement, defensiveness, ego, pressure, and defaults that blind us. Mental clutter clouds our judgment, affecting how we develop as organizers and as human beings. We must learn how to release our preconceived notions before approaching any space we wish to organize.

Take a moment to sit in the room you intend to work on, close your eyes, and feel every emotion or story that comes to mind. In doing this, what arises is often what we're hoping to soothe. If we're establishing systems to "fix" our flaws, the organization will be challenging to sustain. By accepting ourselves and our feelings without letting that view define us, we can create systems that support our needs. Systems that *support* who we are, as opposed to *changing* who we are.

Think of organizing as a support system. If you like working out in your foyer because the light in the morning puts you in a good mood, then move your weights and mat to the entry closet. If you like trying on multiple outfits but don't like putting them back right away, find a discreet holding place for the rejected clothes and designate a time to put them away. If a family is strapped for luggage space, store each person's suitcase in their room and keep their travel toiletries and accessories, like adapters and neck pillows, inside their suitcase. Doing this will create more space in other areas and boost efficiency when it comes time to travel. If you dislike packing lunches daily, get reusable containers and make one or two large batches to meal prep for the week.

Organizing is about understanding behavior and making things readily accessible so those to-do's are more likely to get done. Mindfulness is accepting what is while recognizing the points of frustration or friction that can be easily supported with reasonable systems. Of course, this is easier said than done. It takes time and practice.

PLAYFULNESS

To learn, children are taught to play. We introduce them to building blocks, puzzles, coloring books, and board games because it's easier to learn through play. Playfulness unlocks creativity, self-confidence, and exploration. Young people playing make-believe will instantly flip the script and change every rule and concept, investing all their energy and imagination to form a new world. Nothing is at stake because they are only playing. Playfulness is a form of self-expression. Our responsibility to ourselves, as we enhance our awareness, is to allow our creativity the freedom to roam.

As adults, there is no safer place to play than in our homes, so think of it as a playground to explore, imagine, and change at whim. Be curious, try new things, move things around, and make new connections. Think of the beginning stages of organizing as playing house. Making a mess as you engage with your possessions is an essential step toward getting organized. Indeed, playfulness is the portal to creativity. I use playfulness to experiment with arrangements, often acting them out. For example, by imagining two people in the kitchen doing different tasks, I test the flow before finalizing any new placements of objects.

There's no need to take organizing too seriously. It's not a life-and-death situation. Try not to be too precious about your space or your things. Get messy and live in that space for a day or two, or if you're brave, live in it for a week—or months, depending on what you're tackling. People are often afraid to pull everything out because they're scared they won't be able to get everything back in—but that's the point. Sit with that stuff and figure out what really matters. Being playful in your space evokes creativity and opens up possibilities. Of course, if you get overwhelmed, stop and take a break. Then, when you get back to it, remember this: *Keep what you can care for.*

CRITICAL THINKING

When a space is empty, the potential to create is limitless. Once we fill a space with an idea or an object, we begin to define it. We shape the experience and the outcome. The objects we usher into our spaces, where we place them, and their meaning are products of our thoughts. To create clarity and to assess a situation, we must distance ourselves from them.

Critical thinking is independent thinking. It's not contingent on trends or biases. We are proactive when we are calculating what is before us, identifying the problems, and taking the steps necessary to find solutions. We are not relying on the obvious choice, standard placement, or theory. We are thinking outside the box. When we take time to ponder, *If I put this here, how will I engage with it? How will it affect my actions and others? What habit will it create and how will this habit serve me?*, each question we ask ourselves has the potential to give us a new idea.

To think critically is to gather information and curate a plan that's specific to the unique needs for each space. Identifying habits, previous attempts that were ineffective or effective, the character of any housemates, and the traffic flow are all products of critical thinking. Challenge your judgment of placement and think through the results of your decisions. After all, you are the one who is going to live in the space. So, test your theories, construct and reconstruct different systems, and imagine the possibilities without fear of failure.

Lastly, avoid clinging or attaching to anything you have put into a place. Be willing to adapt, change, and implement new systems when creativity calls for it. Put on your thinking cap.

CONSIDERATIONS WHEN ESTABLISHING SPATIAL AND SELF-AWARENESS

1. **Needs and sensitivities:** Be aware of your own needs. Know the things that make you feel comfortable, safe, and secure. As you prepare to organize your home, use your needs to guide you. Remember, every system you create must support a need. A want is something you can live without; a need is something you must have to live. If you share your space with others, you don't have to organize for their needs and sensitivities all at once. If you are spearheading the project, start with yourself. When the time comes to consider others, invite them to participate, ask them to express their needs, and encourage them to work at cultivating a space that supports them.

    Emotional, mental, and physical sensitivities shape your experiences and needs for a space. If you like a nighttime ritual before bed, create a dedicated space to hold that ritual. If you run on the side of anxiety or depression, clear away some clutter to help reduce the triggers. When homemaking, focus on organizing to support your needs and soothe your sensitivities, rather than chasing any aspirations or aesthetic ideals.

2. **Capacity and limits:** Know your limits. Being overly ambitious is unhelpful. Aspirations are inspiring, but working within your capacity leads to more sustainable

results. Be aware of your capacity, whether related to your time, energy, or budget. Accept whatever level you are at and perform there, trusting you will improve with practice.

Compassionate organizing embraces who we are and where we are today. Don't force the process. Take your time and welcome what each day brings. Ultimately, you set the pace. Not every day is going to be as productive as the last, and that's normal. So long as you're making progress, you will meet your goal.

3. **Saying yes, saying no.** Knowing when to seek help and when to look within is an essential part of canceling the noise. Comparing homemaking rules, methods, and ideologies against your internal wisdom is crucial. Practice affirming suggestions that align with your values and dismissing any that do not.

   It can be difficult to detect the social norms that may be influencing us internally. As you approach your organizing, question why you are putting specific systems into place. Perhaps certain trends are not for you. Say no to anything that is not true to you or for your space. Say yes to being present, creating systems that serve what is in front of you, here and now.

SORTING

In over ten years as a professional organizer, I have never completed a project without first pulling everything out from where it was. While the final stages of organizing are tackled zone by zone, room by room, the process begins with a meticulous sorting—an unearthing of everything related to the issue at hand. This initial phase can be unnerving, chaotic, and uncomfortable—yet it's absolutely necessary. You *must* pull everything out. Even if you believe you know exactly what's inside that box, or that it's inconsequential, empty every bin, every drawer, every nook and cranny.

A better system can't be created within the constraints of the old one. Clear spaces reset our minds and allow us to reassign the placement of things with greater intention. This critical shift begins with sorting.

Sorting is the "like with like" game. We know how to do it, though we don't always *want* to do it. Nevertheless, it's key to the organizing process. Be specific. For instance, separate your salad plates from your dinner plates, mixing bowls from serving bowls, cereal bowls from soup bowls. In the closet, separate the sneakers from the dress shoes, sandals from boots. For those with limited space, this kind of separation is essential. Suddenly, wineglasses and serving platters can be moved to the dining room. Sneakers can relocate from the primary closet to the front hall with other workout gear. Sorting reveals these intricate connections—but to make them, you need a blank slate.

Thorough sorting leads to insightful organizing. If you want new results, you have to be willing to try new approaches. This is not the time to be neat and tidy. This isn't even the time to be thinking about where things should go. Unearth all your things, then sort and divide them. Gain clarity about what you have. Sometimes it helps to lay down a sheet on the floor and put everything there. Make sorting your priority. Think of it as prepping the foundation for solid systems.

CATEGORIZING

After sorting your belongings, the next step is to pair them with similar items. Categories are groups of items with a shared function. We may have had measuring tapes in the linen closet, picture hangers in the office, nails and screws in a kitchen junk drawer, and a hammer on the top shelf of the hall closet. That's a lot of running around to hang a picture. Consolidating similar items eliminates hunting around for objects that serve the same purpose.

Categories are the stepping stones to zones. They are not the zones themselves. Zones are simply the assigned locations for either carrying out a task or storing a related group of items. (I'll explain more later.) For now, think of categories as the contents of a zone. For instance, tools are a category of items that assemble or fix things. Picture hangers and Command strips can also be stationed in the tool category. This category of items may be placed near the utility category, which might include extension cords, batteries, and light bulbs, or alongside the cleaning supplies and laundry category and set in a closet that has a washer and dryer. Collectively, these categories make a zone—they hold a space for the cleaning and maintenance of the home.

When you are creating categories, don't worry about where those things will eventually land. For now, categories can sit wherever is convenient. Focus instead on making logical groupings. Once everything is categorized, you can place it and fine-tune the zone. Right now, you're making connections. If you get stuck in deciding which items complement one another, think out loud as you work: *Why do these things go together? Does this make sense?*

Shifting what you've sorted to form categories may at first feel disorienting. But putting the pieces together is also rewarding. This is a great time to practice mindfulness, playfulness, and critical thinking.

This stage of organizing is tough. Like most things, it gets worse before it gets better. It helps to know that it's not magic that makes it happen. Expect this process to take more time than you think, and make a plan that will keep the household running as smoothly as possible. You don't have to tackle the whole house at once. You might start with the kitchen or home office, before working your way up to the rest of the house. If you stall or start to spiral, go back to decluttering.

* * *

WHEN CLIENTS HIRE Organize With Faith, we give ourselves two to seven days, eight to twelve hours a day, working as a team of three or four people. On one project, I worked for twenty-four hours straight. By the end of the project I was like a zombie. (I do not recommend this.) This work is hard, even for professionals, so be realistic. You might want to think about spending your next vacation organizing your home. It's not a trip to the beach, but the effort you put into it now will greatly serve you and make life easier later.

When we take the time to become a witness to our spaces, to observe how we relate to our possessions, and notice what we have or how we handle it, we begin to see what's happening inside ourselves. Awareness doesn't require that we fix anything. It simply invites us to pay attention. Before we reach for the storage bins or the label maker, let's start with mindfulness, playfulness, and critical thinking.

Remember, what we choose to see is what we can begin to change.

REFLECTIVE QUESTIONS

As you practice cultivating awareness, ask yourself:

- If you live alone, observe your feelings when you spend time in a space. What thoughts arise, and how have they influenced your relationship with your environment?
- If you live with others, what do they perceive as your domestic blind spots? How might these affect the shared living experience?
- In what ways can you incorporate playfulness into your organizing process?
- Recognizing that mess is inherent in organizing, how does living amid purposeful mess make you feel?
- What strategies can you employ to navigate the messiness of organizing and still maintain progress?

The Dos and Don'ts of Organizing

As you embark on this organizing journey, here are a few suggestions:

Do prep with Soul Work and decluttering before you begin organizing.

Do pay attention to how the members of your household navigate each space in the home.

Do ditch the idea of achieving perfection.

Do treat others the way you want to be treated. If you are organizing for someone else, respect their needs and sensitivities.

Don't assume an organizing method that worked for others will work for you.

Don't cling to past placements or systems. What worked before might not work now.

Don't rush the process.

CHAPTER 12

PRINCIPLE TWO: BOUNDARIES

> Boundary: a real or imagined line that marks the limits or edges of something and separates it from other things or places; a dividing line
>
> —*Oxford English Dictionary*

IN CHAPTER 1, I wrote about the day I unpacked all my belongings at the Erwins' house. I sat on the floor with a pile of old journals, tearing out the stories that no longer served me, tossing them in the trash. Technically, I was decluttering, yet it felt more like setting a boundary between my past and my present. I was organizing my thoughts and feelings while organizing my space.

When I look back to that time, I see that I was teaching myself to set boundaries by taking small, deliberate acts. These were not declarations, they were decisions. That season of my life gave me the confidence to start creating space that felt emotionally safe. With every move I've made and every home I've organized since then, I've learned how to set and honor boundaries. The biggest boundary we need to set is often against the narratives we've internalized about who we are and how we should live.

To organize is to establish boundaries. To set a boundary, we must first understand the subtle points and shifts that demarcate a separation. Paying attention to where a point ends and another begins is a critical part of the work.

When we hire an organizer, we're essentially paying them to implement a series of boundaries. As attractive as this may be, our actions are what determine whether the organization will be successful. Systems are only as strong as the measures used to uphold them. Either a lack of boundaries or the presence of them will shape the environment we live in. As organizers and homemakers, our responsibility is to respect the limits we've put into place. When a person fails to maintain boundaries, it compromises the systems and placements that keep a space organized.

Breaking a boundary isn't the end of the world. However, when we lose sight of the lines that give us structure, we pay a price. We feel congested in our space, stressed when things are scattered, anxious and frustrated when we cannot find what we need. Both our mental health and our homes suffer when the boundaries that support us begin to erode. Thus, when we struggle to make sense of a space, we are likely overwhelmed by those unestablished or broken boundaries.

Here are ways to think about the function boundaries have in our lives and homes:

1. **Physical boundaries are the most tangible.** Houses are built with foundations, walls, doors, and thresholds. These are physical cues of separation and purpose. Within the home, we reinforce physical boundaries with the placement of belongings. Our furniture, containers, shelves, and dividers help designate where things go and how a space is meant to function.

2. **Personal boundaries protect our safety and well-being.** They are shaped by what we need, like, or dislike. When they are honored, these boundaries create comfort

and peace. They may not always be visible, but they are grounded in respect. If you share a home, respect other's boundaries. Don't donate belongings without their permission. Asking first is always better than acting without their consent.

3. **Ethical boundaries protect our belief systems.** They highlight our values and affirm our core principles. Organizing within ethical boundaries will foster a mental and spiritual connection to your space. For instance, keeping kosher by having designated dishes is an ethical boundary made visible. Carving out a space to practice salah (prayer), to meditate, or to reflect is also an example of an ethical boundary. Any place or ritual that honors what is meaningful to you serves as an ethical boundary.

These three types of boundaries are interconnected. For instance, a physical boundary may be created to protect an ethical boundary. Though ethical and personal boundaries are often unseen, they guide our decisions, influence our relationships, and shape the way we live.

When a home isn't aligned with someone's ethical or personal boundaries, the discomfort is immediate—even if the space is aesthetically pleasing. For example, for years I grew up in a beautiful home. Still, I was uncomfortable because my personal boundaries weren't respected. Alternatively, although my client Lynn, a practicing Christian and Buddhist, struggled with severe clutter, that wasn't her primary concern. What troubled her most was the emotional and spiritual conflict that clutter caused, along with her desire to live in alignment with her beliefs. Creating more space became a way for her to repair an ethical boundary.

Boundaries can be felt, whether they are visible or not. If a space isn't meeting our needs mentally, emotionally, or spiritually, it's worth investigating why. When we're dissatisfied with some element of our home, it often stems from an internal boundary that has been compromised. This fix might be as simple as relocating items or transitioning a room from one function to another. For example, we may need to turn a closet into a meditation space or repurpose a guest room into a home office. These changes reestablish alignment in who we are, what we value, and how we live.

Organizing is built on a foundation of set boundaries. What one household needs will vary drastically from what another needs. A single person living alone negotiates space differently from how a family of five or two roommates sharing an apartment would do it. Still, the principle remains: Respect the boundaries.

Our boundaries are for ourselves to enforce and follow. If we live alone, it's tempting to dismiss our needs or change systems on a whim. After all, who's watching? Nonetheless, disregarding our boundaries wears out the very structure meant to support us. When we respect the agreements we've made with ourselves and with others, we gain clarity. Organizing then becomes an act of loving ourselves and one another. The boundary is our wish granted.

CONSIDERATIONS WHEN ESTABLISHING BOUNDARIES

1. **Respect the inhabitants' wishes.** Organized systems are rooted in respect. If someone asks that an item be removed from their room because it's not theirs, or no longer serves them, honor that request. Ignoring the request breaks personal boundaries.

However, if someone you love is hoarding and refuses to declutter, recognize that this isn't something you can tackle alone. If the clutter isn't a deal-breaker, seek outside support—an organizer, therapist, or life coach. Talk openly about your mutual needs and find ways to hold space for each other. Clutter often masks underlying pain. Let the clutter be a catalyst for supportive conversations that encourage respect and connection.

That said, if a loved one refuses to change and the environment becomes emotionally and mentally harmful, prioritize your well-being. Remember, space is grace. Giving someone room to deal (or not deal) with their possessions frees you to shape your own life.

2. **Build systems on a solid foundation.** A system based on "someday" is no system at all. Denial about how often—or even if—we'll ever use something will collapse any structure we try to build. If a system is built on a fantasy, it will morph into a nightmare. Hypotheticals pollute our homes, turning dream spaces into stress zones. Entire rooms can get swallowed by "what ifs," leaving no place for things that matter. When we fill spaces with irrelevant items, the organization weakens as a whole. What we need gets buried under what we don't need, making it harder to engage with our belongings.

3. **Assign a purpose to each room.** Clarity about the purpose of a space helps you create systems that support that purpose. The kitchen, for instance, is for nourishment. Items that don't belong there should be moved elsewhere. I used to have a junk drawer in my kitchen until I figured out that

the scissors could go with my office supplies, the batteries and small tools belonged in my utility closet, and the ChapStick could live in my bag. Now, that drawer holds my cooking utensils.

This logic applies to personal spaces, too. If a parent stores their overflow wardrobe in their kid's closet, it infringes on the kid's physical and personal boundaries. The child is left to organize around things that aren't theirs, which disrupts their autonomy and order. When sharing spaces with a partner, family members, or a roommate, define what belongs to whom. You don't have to split everything evenly, just intentionally. One person might take the wardrobe, the other the closet. This alleviates having to be on top of each other in a shared space. Intentional divisions protect the peace, ensuring our personal spaces remain the way we left them.

4. **Embrace the grace period**. At Organize With Faith, we offer a one-week grace period following the work. Clients live with their new systems for a week before we consider the project finished. This allows them time to see if the placement gels. Sometimes we need to come back and modify the systems and placements. Deciding if something works happens only after the organization has been tested. The more likely we are to use the system, the more familiar it becomes and the easier life gets. That does not mean that placements or systems last forever. Things change, and when they do, we go back to Soul Work. However, as long as the system works, we honor it.

* * *

BELOW ARE THE TECHNIQUES I use for guidance, but note that organizing is often a process of trial and error. What works for one space or individual may not work for another. Making adjustments is a necessary component of establishing an effective system.

SPATIAL MAPPING

Spatial mapping is a proactive step that leads to defining zones and placing categories. If you don't have a floor plan, sketch a basic layout of your space. Make note of the activities that occur in each area. Consider the purpose of closets and drawers, their contents, and how they relate to adjacent spaces. Write down which items support the intended function of each area and where they should be placed for optimal utility. This visual map will reveal how rooms function and how major themes connect.

With the spatial map in mind, walk through your home to identify items that don't align with your plan. Question the necessity of those items in their current locations. If they don't serve the designated purpose of the space, relocate them to a more appropriate area or consider letting them go.

ZONING

Zoning involves grouping related categories to facilitate specific tasks. The goal is to position items that contribute to an activity near one another, leading to greater efficiency. For example, in a kitchen, items needed for cooking, baking, and meal prepping should be organized into distinct zones. Fixtures like sinks, ovens, and islands can dictate some natural zones. For instance, their positions might suggest the activities that will occur nearby and the items needed to support those tasks. Zoning is particularly helpful in areas like kitchens, home offices, and playrooms, as it influences the flow of traffic and accessibility.

Furniture placement can also define zones. For instance, an entertainment center housing a TV can also store related electronics, remotes, and games. This may seem obvious, but often such a space will be full of unrelated items, disrupting the intended function of the zone.

Zoning isn't solely where an activity occurs. It can also be about where you retrieve the necessary items. For example, I had a client who enjoyed knitting. Over the years she had accumulated a tremendous amount of yarn and a great number of needles and patterns that she stored throughout the house. Since everything was in multiple locations, she often forgot what she had. By consolidating all her knitting materials in a chest in her office, we created a dedicated zone where she could access and manage her projects. Thus, zones consist of categories that work together to facilitate a specific action. Understanding what you use to execute particular tasks and how you navigate your spaces informs the contents of each zone.

PLACEMENT

A common misconception is that if an item fits into a space, it belongs there. Storing your serveware in a cabinet above the fridge, alongside an old modem router and surplus snacks, may seem convenient, but it undermines the purpose of that storage area. The upper cabinet may be wide enough to accommodate all those unrelated items, but that does not mean they belong there.

Think of organizing like doing a jigsaw puzzle. A piece might seem to fit, but if it's not the correct one, you can't use it to complete the picture. Small concessions to space lead to visible disorder and disrupt the potential of other spaces you wish to organize. Without realizing it, placing items where they do not belong means you cannot account for where they do belong.

Placement conveys an object's importance in the house. If entertaining and making cocktails are part of a homeowner's regular lifestyle, the placement of barware will be front and center. If the homeowner rarely drinks or entertains, the glasses may be stored in a hutch outside of the kitchen or in a cabinet less easily reached. In short, placement can make or break whatever systems we establish, revealing whether they are intuitive or not. If something is in the wrong place, we may never use it or may forget we have it. If jewelry consistently ends up on top of your dresser, put something (like a decorative bowl or basket) there to hold it. If children's toys are always in the living room, consider designating a play area there, rather than having the toys stored somewhere else. Aligning your storage solutions with your natural behaviors promotes sustainable organization.

CONTAINING

When boxes, bins, and baskets are ubiquitous in a space, this perpetuates a desire to overstock. Purchasing a large number of containers to achieve the look of being organized only stokes an infatuation with what that space looks like, rather than how it performs. In many cases, containers become tomblike. We often see things stuffed around and in front of containers left from past organizing attempts. In reality, containers box *us* in if they are relied on too heavily. They rob us of our creativity in reestablishing new systems. When there are too many containers, they shield our mess from critical assessment.

While containers can aid in organization, overreliance on them can lead to clutter and prevent flexibility. Bins and baskets can create the illusion of order, but that doesn't mean we're more organized. Take the dresser drawer. It's filled with T-shirts. You don't need drawer dividers to organize it because the drawer's boundaries are doing their job. Another example is toilet paper that's stacked directly on a shelf or stored in a basket. Either way, the toilet paper is separated from other categories. Some might say storing toilet paper in a basket is less work because they can access it all at once. Another advantage may be a shorter reach to grab it. However, it's rarely the containers that make engagement easy. In the end, it all boils down to the amount you have—having less is always easier to manage.

We are often reluctant to switch things up because of the monetary investment involved and the time spent installing containers. In the end, these purchases are a distraction from the process of organizing. In truth, we do not need to go shopping to create organized systems or spaces. If you organize *before* you shop, and repurpose what you *already have*, you won't need containers. Every shelf, cabinet, drawer, closet, and room is a container, a boundary holding space for your possessions. Instead of defaulting to store-bought solutions, start by reevaluating what you already own.

A common concern is that a big piece of furniture will close in a space. In reality, larger pieces can contain the possessions that makes us feel claustrophobic when we see them. Not only does furniture ground a space but it also houses the systems you make. Repurposing furniture is a great way to mind your budget and house organizing systems. Transforming furniture to suit your needs will take planning and effort. It may even cost you, though the price is often a lot less than buying something new. For instance, add a pole to an old hutch to convert it into an armoire. Or, visit your local lumber yard and get additional shelves to turn that armoire into a freestanding pantry. Move the dresser and turn it into an entryway console to hold hats, gloves, and scarves. Reimagining the furniture in your space can lead to exciting results.

In summary, containers should serve as tools. Avoid letting store-bought containers dictate your organization systems. Instead, declutter, organize, measure, source, and then purchase containers. If you choose to use them, shop with intention, and know that you don't *have* to have them to be organized.

* * *

BOUNDARIES ARE THE ARCHITECTURE of our lives. They define where things end and where we begin. At home, that means being honest about what supports us and what overwhelms us. Setting boundaries doesn't make us rigid, nor does honoring them. Boundaries make us feel grounded, at ease, clear, and secure.

REFLECTIVE QUESTIONS

As you practice honoring your boundaries, ask yourself:

- What are my personal and ethical boundaries?
- How are these boundaries physically represented and supported in my home?
- Have I clearly communicated my boundaries to those I share space with?
- Am I aware of the boundaries of others in my shared space? How do I respect and honor them?
- Have I defined the purpose of each room, and are my belongings appropriately placed to support that purpose?

The Dos and Don'ts of Containers

If you choose to use containers, here are my suggestions:

Do use containers decoratively, in open shelving or glass cabinets, for visual appeal.

Do repurpose existing containers.

Do utilize containers or dividers to separate multiple categories within a single space.

Don't buy containers before determining how you are going to use them.

Don't use containers to store items you don't need or truly want.

Don't rely on containers to hold you accountable. You hold you accountable.

Don't be afraid to take up space. When buying shelves or cabinetry, go longer or taller than you think you need—give your items room to breathe.

CHAPTER 13

PRINCIPLE THREE: ADJUSTMENTS

> Adjustments: small alterations or movements made to achieve a desired fit, appearance, or result—the process of adapting or becoming used to a new situation
>
> —*Oxford English Dictionary*

TIME, infamously out of our control, ushers in seasons that strike and stir us. Moments of monotony morph into periods of radical activity, affecting the systems we once put into place. Consequently, what works today may not work tomorrow.

Time is both a threat and a blessing we face on the organizing journey. It's a threat because even the strongest systems we build will eventually shift, weaken, and break down. It's a blessing because when those systems outlive their usefulness, time invites us to reimagine and rebuild what once was.

The inevitability of impermanence sits at the heart of many people's organizing efforts. Shifts, both incremental and monumental, influence who we are and shape our environment. How we feel about our possessions and our home is constantly in flux, contingent on what is happening within and around us. When a system stops working, it's an opportunity for a new beginning.

Shortly after planting my love garden, I met someone. On our first date, he said, completely sincere, "I love lists. Give me a list of things to do and I'll get them done." I had never been so attracted to a man. A few months later, he was fixing the truck, doing the dishes, cooking, helping me with laundry, rubbing my feet. I thought, *This is too good to be true*. I don't know what kind of flowers my neighbor Beth gave me, but boy, did they work.

Still, I hadn't lived with anyone in over a decade. The idea of sharing space again made me anxious, not because of who *he* was but, rather, because of what I'd experienced in the past. Beyond that, he had two beautiful teenagers he co-parented with their mother. Choosing him meant choosing them. I had curated my spaces for solitude—for *me*. Suddenly, I was sharing cabinets, calendars, and energy. I had to ask myself: *What do I need to feel grounded now?* My answer wasn't a new apartment. It was flexibility.

What followed was a series of adjustments—moving furniture, blending lives, and learning how to share space with intention. Homemaking isn't about locking a space into place. It's about staying open to change and being flexible enough to grow when life invites in something or someone new.

As long as there is space for adjustments, our organizing project becomes a continuum, a gradual transformation with no end. The act of organizing becomes a conversation between us and the events that happen in our lives. Adjustments are our acknowledgment and acceptance of what no longer works, never worked, or is not quite right. With adjustments we also anticipate what is inevitable: the shifts and changes that occur over time.

Personal check-ins strengthen our foundation and help structure the relationship between ourselves and our belongings and space. If the first two principles—awareness and boundaries—support how to make a system, the third principle—adjustments—is how to maintain order. As we approach any system for adjustments, we return to awareness to know how and what to adjust.

When we organize or hire a professional organizer to redo our spaces, the new system seems flawless. There is an unspoken expectation that our efforts will be rewarded with permanency, that what works for now will work forever. A common misconception is that once you get organized, you will stay organized. People do not mentally prepare for the changing seasons, or when a system may fold, or when it no longer works.

Even the most organized people can find themselves disorganized when they resist reassessing, modifying, or leaving a space for change. Adjustments may seem like restless acts—the idea that you must keep moving things around. You may think that the need to adjust means the initial system was flawed. *Neither could be further from the truth.* Adjustments are an empowering aspect of organizing. Adjustments grant us the agency to change what is not working to suit us better, shifting the atmosphere in our favor.

An organized home operates on many connected systems. These attachments form the major networks we rely on to navigate our space. Sometimes the collapse of one part of a network sets off a domino effect, pulling other systems down with it and leaving us living outside the structures we once created. This becomes most apparent when we can't get to the bins or baskets we enthusiastically organized long ago. Networks and systems are interrelated—when one falls, another follows. When they fall, there is an opening to reimagine our space.

When the time comes to make adjustments, three calls to action will alert you.

1. **Friction.** This is the resistance to engage with a system. When we have to overthink where things are, there's a

glitch in the system. When putting things away is a challenge, and getting something out of a closet is a nightmare, that's friction. When things are rubbing together, piled on top of each other, or clustered in front of a system but not integrated into it, that's friction. When a system exists, but friction makes participation unbearable for ourselves and others, it's time for a change. We can perceive friction as frustration, but it's more like an alarm bell. Friction alerts us that something is not working. That alarm can go off in days, months, or years after we have organized. When the contents in the space are too much to maintain, and the room is perpetually in disarray, it's time to make adjustments.

2. **Rites of passage.** Significant events in our lives can provoke transformation. These pivotal moments trigger what we let go of and how we adjust. One example many of us can relate to was the shift to working from home during the global Covid pandemic. Our homes might have functioned on the domestic level, but when a drastic change like quarantine presented itself, adjustments became crucial to adaptation.

   Many things can ignite change: cohabitation, marriage, moving, getting divorced, or the passing of a loved one. Retirement, the birth of a baby, your first single apartment, a career pivot, or downsizing all spur us to do things differently. Monumental moments in our lives influence who we become and what we create. It is tempting and not uncommon to try to replicate systems that worked previously, yet this is often unsuccessful. Adjusting to a new space or lifestyle is a mindful act. Practice awareness during these times to help build something unique. Occasionally, our systems are solid enough to withstand a rite of passage. In this case, drastic changes don't apply. Still, the organization will demand modifications to support the evolution.

3. **High-activity bearing and impact zones.** Not all rooms carry the same weight. Kitchens, mudrooms, entryway closets, and home offices will often absorb the full force of our daily lives. These spaces are liable to turn into parking lots for random belongings. The result? Clutter. When every corner is working overtime, the space will fall out of balance. This happens when too many categories dominate one area or zone, without balancing less active spaces.

   As organizers, we decide how much an area is used and relied upon, based on what we place there. If an area is bustling with activity, and therefore difficult to maintain, adjusting the placement of things to disperse that activity will help. Review highly active areas to pinpoint whether specific zones or categories can be moved, so as to offset the imbalance of engagement throughout the house.

Resolving places that are affected by friction, rites of passage, or high-activity bearing and impact zones reinvigorates our homes. An overactive space will tatter even the best systems. If we're exhausted from picking up misplaced items, enduring a life change, or feeling unmotivated, it's time to make adjustments.

* * *

AFTER WE HAVE COMPLETED our organizing projects, we always benefit from a grace period. Carving out a number of days to remain focused on the effects of using our new systems will unveil whether they truly work. During this time, we test their durability, efficiency, and efficacy to determine if modifications are necessary. Adjustments are not busy work—we must change only what is necessary. We may feel tempted to start from scratch. Instead, identify what is not working and ask yourself why it is not.

Often, a small glitch can be fixed by moving a few things around. Isolated adjustments unlock the potential of a system, and here specificity is key. *Leave what works alone.* Make an assessment of what is not working, and with a clear directive in mind, employ modifications to address that specific area. Indeed, modifications are hard to make when we are married to an idea, aesthetic, or placement. Admiration blinds our ability to troubleshoot. Be open and flexible when approaching the task of modifications. Being prepared to make changes to what's been done will make us better organizers.

Degrees of Adjustments

Adjustments keep the integrity of our work intact. They refine the systems we create, but they are not the system itself. As we explore adjustments, imagine the system as a rubber band. Testing the elasticity of each system can make obvious a slight extension or a broader use, depending on need.

If a placement does not feel right, or the engagement is not there, extend the system, stretching it to accommodate your needs. You can relocate categories or replace zones. However, know that every system can be stretched only so far before reaching a breaking point. Once the system is broken, rebuilding is required. The various degrees of adjustments prevent that disorganization. Apply the appropriate gradation to best suit the obstacle you face.

MAINTENANCE

Maintenance is that rubber band at rest, when tidying up is all that's needed. Maintenance is the acknowledgment that a system works well and serves as is. Every system requires maintenance. Things are returned to their respective places, refolded, or spruced up.

When I say, *keep what you can care for*, I mean what you can maintain. Sew on the buttons that are missing from a jacket, fix the door hinge that is loose and causing the door to tilt, reupholster the chair you inherited from your great aunt, print and frame the pictures and then hang them rather than having them sit on the floor. Schedule to get the rugs steamed, remove that stubborn stain that is stopping you from wearing your favorite shirt. Take your VHS and old camcorder tapes to the audio shop to get them digitized. Spend your money taking care of the things you own, as opposed to buying new things to contain them.

When I work with clients, I find that much of what is taking up their space are abandoned projects—their to-do lists remaining in limbo. Completing your projects is a crucial component in getting your home in order. Don't let outstanding projects obstruct your ability to maintain the systems you've created.

Seasonal changes, holidays, and hosting events are excellent occasions to tidy up. As you housekeep, take the opportunity to beautify your systems. Maintenance is organizational housework—nothing changes, but everything shines.

MODIFICATIONS

Modifications can trigger substantial results over time. Modifications are moderate stretches of that rubber band. When using new systems, we quickly determine whether or not they are working. The moment we realize something is not working, we need to recognize what has to change and make the modification. Do not be afraid to tweak your system. Every item you move will dictate a different engagement. If you choose to make modifications, execute them after you're clear on what you're changing and why.

Not all adjustments are grand gestures. Often, modifications are about preference—the difference between having your cutting board near the sink or beside the range. Or, whether you prefer to keep your vitamins and supplements in the bathroom or in the kitchen.

A few tweaks to an organized space can determine whether you engage a system or not. Think of modifications as the solution to any organizing hiccups.

REVISIONS

Revisions are full stretches of the rubber band—as far as it will go. We are not breaking the system, but we are going beyond modifications. Revisions tend to come after a system has degraded over a few years or when rites of passage make them necessary. Revisions require an element of new spatial mapping. To pull off a revision without totally dismantling our systems, we must identify what needs to be relocated.

For example, in my current apartment, I lack closet space. For years, I kept my coats in my guest room/home office closet. When my partner moved in, I had to make space for his things. My bedroom had a small closet for my clothes and a back room where I used to meditate. The back room had a nice-sized window and lots of natural light. Over the years, I'd routinely do my makeup in there, and I'd spritz on some perfume before going out. While brainstorming where to move my coats, I realized my meditation room was evolving. I could keep what I loved most—having a place to reflect and pamper myself—while still solving my spatial dilemma. I mounted shelves in the back room, put up a rod, and purchased a beautiful wardrobe to store clothes, accessories, and makeup. I kept a floor pillow and brass singing bowls nearby so that I could still meditate in my new dressing room. I relocated my coats to the bedroom closet, and I moved my partner's clothes into the guest room closet. While the focus was on making space for my partner and his things, I was able to revise the placement of some of my wardrobe in a way that worked better for me.

REORGANIZATION

At this point, the rubber band has snapped. No amount of maintenance or tweaks can revive what once was. When a system breaks, we've either disengaged partially or abandoned it altogether. There is no longer a connection between us and the system—or the system and the network to which it once belonged.

When you feel inundated with stuff and overwhelmed by what surrounds you; when things don't have a home; when you cannot find objects and don't have a grasp on what you have; all this is a sign that the space needs an overhaul. After years of inhabiting a space, we cannot always see it as it truly is. It becomes easy not to see the clutter.

If you can't see clutter, pay attention to how you feel in the space. Are you inspired, energized, feeling creative, and contented, or are you anxious, overwhelmed, frustrated, and depressed? Emotions indicate when it's time to go back to Soul Work, declutter, and reorganize.

* * *

WHEN CONCRETE IS POURED TO make sidewalks, the space between each square allows for the inevitable expansion and contraction as the material solidifies and settles. The squares have space to breathe as they weather the elements, bear the pressure of foot traffic, and take the weight of bikes and strollers. Thanks to that space, the concrete responds with minimal cracking. In other words, it is hard to break what bends.

The construction and deconstruction of the systems we put in place should be able to withstand the seasons of life. When we are flexible with the systems we create and the changes life presents, organizing becomes a way to reconnect. Adjustments are a sign we're evolving. When we stay flexible in life, and particularly at home, we're open to love, growth, and renewal. Adjusting isn't giving up control. It's choosing to meet the moment with grace.

Maintenance, modifications, revisions, and reorganization assist in improving what we have created, and they serve in fine-tuning our techniques. Any degree of adjustment will foster an intimate relationship with change, flexibility, and evolution. As we practice adjusting our work, we become aware of our organizing blind spots and potential pitfalls. Repairing these glitches hones our organizing skills. Additionally, adjustments help us discern when it is time to let things go and reimagine the potential of a space. As we practice welcoming this certainty, we level up as organizers.

If something feels imbalanced, it's our responsibility to recalibrate. Processing the inevitable obstacles that occur over time keeps us in harmony with our homes and lives.

REFLECTIVE QUESTIONS

As you prepare to make adjustments and welcome change in your life, ask yourself:

- What recent events have prompted a need for change or adjustments in my life?
- Which areas of my home are most affected by high activity, and what adjustments can redistribute traffic and reduce clutter?
- How does my relationship with change reflect my attachment to possessions and their roles in my life?
- What can I do to better embrace change?

The Dos and Don'ts of Adjustments

Do keep up the maintenance of your home and your organized systems.

Do approach organizing with a sense of flexibility and openness to change.

Do use the adjustment phase as a moment to bring yourself back to spatial and self-awareness.

Don't ignore places of friction. Instead, use them as an indication to reassess your space.

Don't hesitate to go back to Soul Work and decluttering.

* * *

IN PART THREE, we examine how race, gender, and class have come to define the notion of domesticity, as well as the unattainable ideal of perfection. We also explore the history, cultural mores, and social structures that surround domesticity in America. Reframing what we've been taught restores balance to how we think about and experience homemaking and one another.

PART THREE

SOCIAL WORK

CHAPTER 14

SEASONS OF CHANGE

EVERY SEASON ARRIVES and departs in its own time. We may experience seasons of rest that quickly morph into activity. A season of Soul Work gives way to a season of letting go. A season of releasing clears the path for a season of renewal. Every season carries its own assignment. This cyclical rhythm commands respect. As painful or as joyful as it may be to experience, time always delivers change. It's up to us to accept the call—to lean in with faith, participate intently, and trust that what feels disruptive may end up being transformative.

We may not get to choose the seasons we're in. We do, however, get to choose how we greet those seasons. When change arrives, we have two choices for how to engage with it:

Be passive. Rest. Wait. Watch. Listen.

Be active. Decide. Plan. Build. Speak.

Seasons of change gift us with insight. They teach us about the highs and lows, the opposites that play off each other to make us whole. In truth, you can't have joy without sadness or loss without gain. Life is not black or white. It has a depth and a range that bleed into each other for a greater purpose.

We've grown accustomed to thinking that life will adjust to us. That it moves at the pace of our preference. That we can dismiss the inevitability of change and remain in the seasons we like best. Yet, change is not a threat. It's a promise. When we resist it, we disrupt balance.

In nature, when something falls out of balance, the earth responds by shedding, shifting, and redistributing so that life can continue to flourish. These moments may seem like the end of the world, but nature appears to operate with a wisdom we often struggle to comprehend. *Everything is connected.* If Mother Nature teaches us anything, it's that the whole is the sum of its parts. For the whole to function, and even to thrive, balance is required. Beauty and evolution come from honoring difference and embracing change.

* * *

WE MUST CHALLENGE the idea of homemaking as something existing solely for ourselves. We need community to thrive. When we begin to understand that our homes are not separate from the world, we start to see that cultivating awareness, boundaries, and adjustments holds the potential for *collective restoration*. If we can reimagine our homes with honesty, acceptance, and grace, we can reimagine our society in the same way.

As we learn how to make adjustments, we are doing more than personal work. We are engaging in *political* work. Through Home Work, we make space for Social Work. This rocky terrain is where personal responsibility meets collective change. In order to make collective change, we must turn outward, toward the shared space we are shaping together. It's time for us to reckon with the stories we've inherited about homemaking. We need to examine who performs it presently and who has done it historically. We need to question what domesticity has taken from some of us and given to others. In a country tangled in conversations about race, class, gender, and capitalisim, domesticity is the thread that binds the culture together.

* * *

A FEW YEARS AGO, I was interviewed by a lifestyle writer. She was writing an article on kitchen organization and she was using her kitchen as the example. I was giving her organizing advice via Zoom. From the start, she immediately apologized for the state of her home. She opened her cabinets, embarrassed by what looked to me like a normal kitchen. She said, "I watch these shows and read articles hoping to find the answers as to why my house isn't organized. And I end up feeling like I'm not doing it right, like I'm missing something."

I stared at the computer screen thinking, *What on earth is this woman talking about? Sure, some zones could be tightened, some systems improved, but there's nothing to apologize for.*

"No matter how hard I try, I can't get it right," she continued. "I know women who have perfect homes. But I'm not one of them. I wasn't born organized. My brain doesn't work that way." She told me about her anxiety and her battles with depression. She wondered if that was why she couldn't keep her space organized. She asked if I thought getting organized would soothe her mind.

"It depends," I told her. "If you think of organizing as a way to attain perfection, achieve happiness, or be like others, it may very well be the source of your anxiety." I shared with her my concerns that organizing with that goal becomes a rigid, shallow pursuit of a fantasy. Organizing is sold to us in the media as aspirational, but what exactly are we taught to aspire to?

Our culture has stripped homemaking of its power and has convoluted it with rainbows, shopping sprees, sparks of joy, and the fear that if it's not swift and fun, we'll end up on the TV series *Hoarders*. These extremes blind us from finding balance. Balance comes from accepting where we're at and what we're working with. It means designing a home that's authentic to us. I have no doubt that bringing more order to one's life can soothe anxiety, but only if the process and outcome aren't done in comparison to someone else. We can admire, respect, or be inspired by others—and still be at peace with the home we've made.

Originally, this journalist wanted to write about how emotional trauma shows itself in our spaces. Further, how her depression and anxiety resulted from her fixation with domestic perfection. Instead, she was assigned to write about spice jars and risers.

"If these stories don't resonate with you, why keep writing them?" I asked.

Her answer was simple. "They go gangbusters, and advertisers love them. Editors request them, even if they're all the same."

I would soon learn that it was a numbers game. That most shelter magazines wanted product links—a solution to clutter in the form of stuff. But there isn't a product sold for Soul Work. Yet when we organize our thoughts, and we explore how we feel about our relationship to our possessions, values, and society, our perspective of what matters shifts exponentially.

Our aspirations reach beyond what's seen in the media, which depicts and brands the home as affluent, feminine, and materialistic. Domesticity is sold as a lifestyle, when in reality it's labor—disproportionate, unpaid, emotional, and physical labor that is shouldered by women, who remain largely invisible and rarely acknowledged.

While the burden of domestic labor has historically fallen on women, everyone on some level experiences it, depends on it, and participates in it. Domesticity impacts us all. Homemaking is a communal project, built and sustained across races, genders, and class lines. It is where we collide as people, offering our varied contributions to something we all connect with.

After my interview with the journalist, I started to wonder, *Do we actually love this domestic content, or is it all we've ever known?* Indeed, it's the only lens we've been given. These spaces may inspire us, but they are *all* the same, performed in a way that undermines our emotional reality and, for many of us, our lived experiences. Time after time, I have watched this tension simmer: what we want, what we need, and what truly makes us feel at home, versus what we're sold—containers for our stuff. Pristine spaces modeled by pristine women.

I started thinking about that representation. What happens when we don't see diversity realistically reflected in our culture? I thought of how fragmented we are as a society and how difficult it is to embrace homemaking holistically. If we know that homemaking isn't as simple as it looks in the media, why are we so enamored of it? Perfection in the home and garden industry is never marketed as unique. Who benefits from that fantasy? What is the cost of chasing it?

My friend Matthew always jokes, saying, "Once you see it, you can't unsee it." He repeats this whenever he has a bad date or a ridiculous encounter at work. As much as I roll my eyes when he says it, there is truth in it. In my early years as a professional organizer, topics I hadn't considered before stood out glaringly as I attempted to expand my reach. The more I lived, the more I learned. I started noting the stark difference between what's shown in the media and what's happening at my clients' homes. I'd call friends, ranting about yet another upper-class woman with no previous experience in the professional field of domesticity (other than being a woman) teaching us how to make things look pretty. I started researching the history of homemaking to substantiate arguments I was having, mostly with myself. I began to feel disappointed and embarrassed by my industry.

One night over dinner, a friend asked me, "If you don't like it, why do you do it?"

"It's tricky. I like the work and I've met a lot of wonderful people.

I enjoy organizing. I like the challenge of walking into a space and figuring it out. I could do it all day long, but I don't like the obsession with spaces having to look a particular way. I don't like the expectation that there won't be any emotional work or effort involved in maintaining our belongings. And I don't like how *white* it is. I hate that I'm a part of an industry that is so blatantly exclusive. It's a miracle I've made it this far."

I was feeling boxed in by the selling of illusions that strip people of their common sense. I no longer wanted to be silent about how this industry has refused to acknowledge women like me. Women who have been keeping house for years, for generations. Women who are the backbone of this profession. Who may not look a certain way or fit a particular ideal, yet hold knowledge and expertise that's been shaped by their experiences and enriched through their diversity.

When you love something, there comes a moment when you want more from it. You know it can evolve, make space for a fresh perspective, find a new way of being in the world. You have faith in what you've poured your time, energy, and heart into—after all, you're part of the reason it exists. So, when it doesn't change and adjustments aren't on the table, you have to make a choice.

You have to answer the call.

My power isn't defined by an ability to mimic mainstream ideals. It's from the courage to question them. Social Work begins with reclaiming the cultural narratives that have long been dismissed and honoring the homes that reflect our flawed yet beautiful humanity. Real homemaking—true, authentic homemaking—is vulnerable work. It's Soul Work and it's Social Work. It calls on us to face ourselves, confront our failures, and recognize our shared struggles. Only then can we dismantle the barriers of race, class, and gender to make space for a new way of viewing our homes.

REFLECTIVE QUESTIONS

As you reflect on how media has shaped your relationship to domesticity, ask yourself:

- What does it mean to make my home part of a collective good rather than an isolated achievement?
- What ripple effect might my personal transformation have on society?
- How does the lack of diversity in the home industry disrupt social balance?
- What have I internalized from the media's portrayal of "perfect" homes and "perfect" homemakers?

CHAPTER 15
OPPORTUNITY DENIED

I USED TO BELIEVE that home was purely personal—an intimate endeavor. That the way we keep our homes was separate from society's deeper tensions. However, homemaking as a business has always reinforced America's complicated divisions. The politics of housekeeping, homemaking, and organizing were revealed when I hit the invisible barrier preventing women like me from reaching the same professional heights as others. There was only so much I could do or be when it came to the business of the home. That is, there was a formula for selling homemaking that I did not fit. Even with all my experience, I'd neglected to examine the cultural history of domesticity—how societal norms have shaped our expectations of who housekeeps and how. This realization led me to see the bigger picture of how the home is more than a private sanctuary. It is where identity, power, and history intersect.

* * *

I STILL REMEMBER having a heated argument with my father. A comment he made at that time wounded me: "You think you're doing something Black women haven't been doing since slavery? You ain't doin' nothing but cooking and cleaning up after white people. You're no different than Vera."

Vera, my paternal grandmother, smoked like a chimney and had jet-black skin that was offset by striking silver hair. She was tough as nails. Nothing about her was warm or inviting. She was a single mother who inherited land from her stepfather, built her forever home, and planted peach trees out back. Vera was a housekeeper for upper-class families. She worked for the Newmans, a group of cattle ranchers in California, for over thirty years. They were kind people. They gave her a deep freezer and gifted her a steer every Christmas to fill it. Her entire life revolved around the Newmans and keeping her little house on the corner of Brown Street.

My father's words were painful and confusing because there was some truth in them. I could argue that I was making a meaningful difference, yet that alone didn't separate me from other domestics, from the countless women who cleaned houses, organized kitchens, cooked, laundered, and maintained the homes of others. His comparison of my work to Vera's wasn't simply a personal criticism: It highlighted a historical stereotype I hadn't fully confronted.

For years, his judgment stayed with me until I realized there *is* a fundamental difference between Vera and me. This isn't work I *have* to do. It's work I *choose* to do. Though we are generations apart, I carry her legacy forward, insisting that domestic labor be respected, and profitable—no matter who performs it.

* * *

"BLACK WOMEN BEEN KEEPING HOUSE for years, and I'm not keeping house, I'm changing house." Those were the opening lines to my sizzle reel—a high-energy promotional video, much like a movie trailer—for a homemaking show that, if picked up, would launch *Organize With Faith* onto television. As I stood on a Manhattan sidewalk, reluctant to twirl for the camera, I realized what I was being asked to do wasn't about organizing, or even housekeeping. It was about performing an ideal of domesticity.

The opportunity had been presented to me by my client Frank, who developed reality TV shows. After submitting the reel, I was ushered into a meeting with executives who worked in offices with sweeping city views. Frank thanked me for curtailing his clutter, then candidly said, "As a Black man, I have to ask you: How does it feel being a Black woman doing this type of work for wealthy white women?" His wife was white, as were most of my clients. While making the sizzle reel, the director had asked me a similar question about working in the homes of white women. The question had never crossed my mind because, while organizing, I hadn't experienced feeling Black in a white space. It was only in that moment that I was distinctly aware of my race in a predominantly white industry.

The next meeting echoed the first. Following the small talk and compliments, the VP leaned in apologetically. "You know, you're Black. Our audience doesn't respond favorably to Black hosts." Before I could process his bluntness, he added optimistically, "Who knows, you might be the one to change that." I thanked him for the meeting and walked out. As I passed posters on the walls promoting countless networks and multiple shows, there wasn't a single one showing a host of color.

I hadn't watched design shows or consumed enough home and garden content to witness its prejudices. From that day onward, I couldn't help seeing things differently. In the real world, the home and garden industry is diverse. Businesses and professions such as architecture, design, construction, landscaping, and housekeeping are rich with immigrants. Black people, Asians, Mexicans—both women and men—are collaborating to design, build, and maintain spaces to withstand the test of time. People of color are ubiquitous in domestic occupations—yet they are hardly ever seen in the media.

After that last meeting with producers, I focused on growing my business. Friends in the entertainment industry consoled me, explaining that these things were all about timing. Here's the thing about glass ceilings: They let you glimpse the possibilities clearly, with those opportunities dangling just beyond reach. You can't always see the world you're soaring into until you collide, painfully, like a bird hitting a spotless window. There may not be "Whites Only" signs anymore, but division persists in subtler ways.

What's most compelling about the home and garden industry is its success in selling contrived joy: happiness devoid of context, as though joy could ever exist without complexity, flaws, mess, and history. It's astonishing how popular this prefabricated happiness has become—that beauty and intentionality can exist only within the bounds of conformity. It's as if joy can't coexist with truth, regardless of how painful that truth is. Yet, this is the reality that Black people live every day. We choose joy not in spite of our history but *alongside* it. That choice, in a world that has tried to diminish us, becomes its own kind of resistance.

Representation isn't merely about what viewers *want* to see. It's also what viewers *ought* to see. Diversity, visibility, equality, and inclusion all shape how audiences relate to themselves and one another. Throughout my career, I have made multiple sizzle reels, fielded countless inquiries, and sat through numerous phone calls and meetings for ways to promote my brand. Yet some opportunities that initially seemed inevitable, even destined for me, eventually faded. Perhaps it isn't true that audiences don't respond favorably to Black hosts. It could also be that audiences don't respond favorably to inauthentic content.

To date, the lack of diversity in the media's home renovation, real estate, interior design, and organizing content prevails: *Flip or Flop*, *Christina on the Coast*, *Everything But the House*, *The Laundry Guy*, *Bargain Mansions*, *Farmhouse Fixer*, *Property Brothers*, *Good Bones*, and *Dream Home Makeover*. These provide no hosts of color. If film and TV are presented as more diverse now than ever before, why is this particular genre so white?

* * *

IN 2020, HGTV, which is headquartered in Knoxville, Tennessee, became one of the most influential cable networks, reaching 60 million viewers.[1] In 2015, their annual revenue totaled more than a billion dollars in advertising and licensing fees, paid by companies endorsed by the network. This domestic ecosystem created more than design and home-renovation content. A new wave of cult domesticity stimulated consumerism, while perpetuating division.

Amid the national unrest following George Floyd's murder, the network publicly acknowledged its lack of diversity. "We have probably not done the best job regarding our talent," admitted HGTV president Jane Latman.[2] *Vanity Fair* reported that tangible changes were coming, highlighting upcoming shows that would feature Black hosts, such as *$50K Three Ways* with Tiffany Brooks and *Sister Fixers* hosted by Howard graduates Leslie Antonoff and Courtney Robinson. Despite the promises, *Sister Fixers* never aired, and *$50K Three Ways* didn't get a second season.

The following year, for Black History Month, HGTV released a promotional campaign showcasing Black talent. Hosts like Egypt Sherrod of *Married to Real Estate* and Page Turner of *Fix My Flip* spoke passionately about inclusion. "I see the progress, I feel the progress, I read the progress, I experience the progress—this is part of history, where you see a network say, this is our standard, this is our platform, this is who we are, and we are inclusive of everybody," Turner evangelized.[3]

I found the commercial so compelling that I replayed it three times. I, too, had been blinded by what *Vanity Fair* said is described by some as "harmless fluff, soothing, and diverting entertainment free of all the prickly politics of the outside world."[4] Yet, in 2022, only about 8 percent of HGTV's hosts were Black, with a marginal increase when co-hosting alongside white counterparts. Shows with biracial hosts paired with white co-hosts had significantly more airtime than shows hosted solely by Black talent.

In 2022, the top twenty shows playing on HGTV had white hosts (with the exception of *100 Day Dream Home*, in spot 11 with interracial couple Brian and Mika).[5] To put this into perspective, within the year, *Home Town* got roughly 755 hours, sometimes playing for fifteen hours in one day. Meanwhile, *Fix My Flip* had roughly 67 hours of play time.

This lack of visibility inhibits the host's potential endorsements, as well as opportunities for franchises and lifespan on the network. For viewers, the lack of variety may impact who they favor to hire for their own home-improvement projects. Limited representation on a platform as influential as this thus exemplifies a longstanding prejudice.

Beyond its hosts, it also appears that this genre fails to progress diversity on the back end. Based on information publicly available to us, Black people in production, writing, directing, and editing look bleak. When these narratives make their way into print, in magazines like *Southern Living*, *Country Living*, *Better Homes & Gardens*, *House Beautiful*, *Real Simple*, *Good Housekeeping*, and *Taste of Home*, the vision of domesticity is overwhelmingly filtered through white editorial leadership. This bias shapes not only what is seen but also what is valued.

However, the homebuyers who participate in the shows are diverse. BIPOC (Black, Indigenous, People of Color) couples flood the scenes to purchase homes or undertake major renovations. In addition, the commercials render inclusivity—a kaleidoscope of actors appear in Walmart, Home Depot, and Wayfair ads, enticing viewers to buy their goods. Nevertheless, there is a difference between seeing a diverse population as consumers and viewing them as leaders. The romanticization of domesticity in the media rests on an age-old blueprint that robs non-whites of recognition as agents in this field. More important, it oversimplifies the traumatic territory of homemaking in America.

Southern hospitality remains HGTV's sweet spot. Southern values are branded in the rapid success of shows like *Fixer Upper* and *Home Town*. The term "Southern hospitality" dates as far back as the 1830s, but this doesn't mean Southerners were exceptionally hospitable during this time. Rather, the term emerged as political propaganda during escalating tensions about slavery between the North and the South.[6] According to Anthony Szczesiul, author of *The Southern Hospitality Myth*, Southern states intentionally branded themselves as the authority on homemaking and hospitality, promoting "a sense of transregional white community, solidarity, and privilege." Szczesiul explains that the Southern hospitality myth consistently portrays Black Americans (I would also include immigrants and people of color) as either invisible or an alien population, incapable of being assimilated into mainstream culture.[7]

The South's legacy continues to shape America's home narratives. In the view of many, myself included, the sanitized portrayal of Southern life, as seen on HGTV, echoes a tradition of domestic fantasy—one that can be traced back to publications like *The Progressive Farmer*.

* * *

THE PROGRESSIVE FARMER, founded in 1886 by an ex-Confederate colonel, was an agricultural bible that highlighted livestock, agriscience, home life, and recipes catering to rural Southerners. As the farming population decreased with growing industrialization, the magazine's readership also steadily declined. By the time of the Civil Rights movement, the magazine struggled to stay relevant. It was phased out and replaced with *Southern Living* magazine.

Southern Living was introduced in the October 1963 issue of *The Progressive Farmer*, with a cover depicting a serene image of a white boy resting against a barn, with a calf lying peacefully in his lap.[8] At the time, Birmingham, Alabama, where the magazine was headquartered, was dominating the national headlines for its illegal and inhumane opposition to integration. Two weeks before *Southern Living*'s debut, four Black girls died in the 16th Street Baptist Church bombing. "The blood of our little children is on your hands," Martin Luther King Jr. telegrammed the governor of Alabama, George Wallace.[9] While politicians and activists scrambled to find a resolution, the concept of Southern hospitality emerged again.

"Southern people were thirsting for something to make them feel good about themselves," publisher Emory Cunningham recounted.[10] Each page of the magazine highlighted the region's finest attributes, natural resources, and breathtaking homes and plantations. At the same time, a *Better Homes & Gardens*'s 1963 ad boldly declared, "Get your cotton pickin' hands off that lint dryer,"[11] implying modern technology could seamlessly replace the historical labor of Black domestic workers. The white models in the advertisements demonstrated the work of vacuum cleaners, dishwashers, and washing machines. In editorial content, these white women arranged flowers, made crafts, cooked, and decorated all by themselves. Decade after decade, page after page, the magazines showed manicured white people doing it all.

This selective portrayal of domesticity exemplified what scholar Tara McPherson calls "lenticular logic," allowing conflicting realities to coexist without interaction.[12] For the South to be seen as aspirational, images of Black people had to be erased. In other words, while the media covered the heinous hate crimes happening during the Civil Rights movement, *Southern Living* doubled down on an idealized vision of domestic life.

For Black people in America, domestic tasks such as cooking, cleaning, sewing, serving, and child-rearing represented their earliest forms of employment, alongside farming. After emancipation, the dynamics of domestic labor shifted but they remained unequal. By 1860, the majority of free Black women worked as domestic servants. In Southern cities like Atlanta, legal barriers—including required letters of recommendation—made it difficult for Black domestics to leave exploitative households. According to historian Enobong Hannah Branch, only in the South did Black women constitute a significant contingent of domestic workers.[13] Most white women in the region refused to enter the occupation because of its association with slavery.

In regions beyond the South, domestic labor was done by immigrant women, predominantly Irish and Eastern Europeans, while native-born white women pursued new opportunities in manufacturing, clerical, and teaching roles. The Great Migration brought Black families northward in hopes of safer living conditions and better wages, yet they encountered similar exploitative treatment.[14] Discrimination continued to limit Black women's access to better-paying positions and perpetuated domestic service as a family tradition that was passed from mothers to daughters. During the Great Depression, competition for work increased. Black domestics for hire lined up on street corners and in empty lots in the northernmost part of New York City, an area that became known as the Bronx Slave Market.[15]

As white women continued to progress in various careers, conspicuous consumption and the showcase of the middle-class lifestyle began to take root. Consequently, the uptick in Black and Brown maids cemented their station as domestic servants.

During World War II, the Bracero Program—an agreement

between Mexico and the United States—facilitated Mexican employment in America's railroad and farming industries. Millions of Mexican citizens moved to the states for these jobs.[16] Even though the Bracero contracts were issued only to men, there was still a demand in America for female migrant labor.[17] As women and children moved north to reunite with their loved ones, some found work farming while others poured into garment and domestic labor trades. By the 1960s, Mexican girls and women dominated housekeeping positions in Texas, California, and the Southwest.[18]

Thus, America's image of homemaking only exists because of the invisible labor of Black, Brown, and immigrant women. The mainstream media still deny BIPOC experts the opportunity to redefine homemaking etiquette. However, the rise of social media has enabled marginalized groups to showcase their domestic expertise authentically and directly to the public. Audiences increasingly seeking genuine representation and inclusion are turning away from the traditional media and turning toward online content created by everyday innovators.

One notable example is TikTok's Queen of Clean, a Mexican American housekeeper who rose to prominence during the pandemic by sharing her short, practical videos of cleaning routines. Her content went viral, earning millions of views and lucrative sponsorships.[19] Indeed, her success underscores how social media has begun to revitalize our perceptions of domestic labor. With or without network backing, BIPOC professionals are claiming new space and building new audiences. What was once dismissed as a menial occupation is gradually gaining recognition.

* * *

WHEN I WAS IN MIDDLE SCHOOL, my mama introduced me to the movie *Gone with the Wind*. I remember being pleasantly surprised by the sight of Black people on the screen. Out of all the classic films we watched on TV, this one was by far the most visibly "diverse." However, the Black people on the screen were depicted as stupid, lazy, and childlike. Mammy, played by Hattie McDaniel, was the exception. She was big-boned and exaggerated. She barked when she spoke and moved fearlessly through the scenes. Her bond with Scarlett O'Hara was familial. Mammy had raised generations of white children and had managed the home, all tasks that demanded organization, time management, and expertise. Yet when Hattie McDaniel accepted her Oscar for the role, she was criticized for reinforcing stereotypes. She replied, "I'd rather play a maid than be one," which made me wonder: *Is it the work that's demeaning, or is it the social contempt toward the immigrants and people of color who do it?*

I recently watched *Gone with the Wind* again, and I counted the many times Mammy was mocked, dismissed, and patronized. I called my mother and asked her why they treated Mammy unjustly in the film. I asked her why domestics are often laughed at and positioned as comedic relief, or portrayed as non-experts in a field they know well.

"They laugh because they don't want us to know how powerful we are. You know that saying? 'The hand that rocks the cradle is the hand that rules the world.'"

Strangely enough, *Gone with the Wind* reminded me of a show in the early 2000s called *Clean House*, which aired alongside shows like *Trading Spaces* and *What Not to Wear*. *Clean House* arrived on the scene before hoarding was widely accepted as a compulsive disorder. The show ran for ten seasons, and nine of those seasons were hosted by the incomparable Niecy Nash in the company of Trish, the organizer; Matt, the handyman; and Mark, the interior designer. Together, they tackled America's messiest homes.

Nash, a tell-it-like-it-is confidante, provided comedic relief for a tender subject. She was loud, maternal, and sassy, doling out doses of tough love. She also bore the brunt of her castmates' jokes. In one episode, they dressed up to mimic Nash, wearing wigs, rolling their necks, pointing their fingers, and smacking their lips. Yet, Nash was the star of the show. She brought depth to a sensitive topic, subtly moving it emotionally forward. Her knowledge and intuition in guiding participants out of disarray were irreplaceable. Shortly after she left, the show was canceled.

* * *

IN AN ERA OF COOKIE-CUTTER homemaking shows, I yearn for greater diversity on all fronts. There's so much more to unpack than just watching renovations. There's more to transforming a home than the final "reveal." I want to see something on television that resembles real life. Experts in the domestic fields are BIPOC and immigrants who teach us how to landscape, build homes, do our laundry, housekeep, take care of our children, and organize our lives. I want to be whisked away, not to some million-dollar mansion but to a space kept by those who know what it takes to make a house a home. I would welcome gratitude for, and recognition of, the lineage of women who have spent years turning down beds, dusting furniture, and tidying up homes they historically could never own.

Too often, people from different backgrounds, cultures, and faiths are portrayed as "others," with their perspectives on homemaking denied. Yet, highlighting the history and heritage of people from various identities broadens our perception of domesticity.

If we are going to talk about home, we can't divorce it from the current state of the world. When we romanticize the idea of domesticity in America, we quietly endorse all aspects of it, from the seemingly innocent and ubiquitous white home organizers, real estate brokers, and interior design duos to the more aggressive forces of redlining, gentrification, and segregation.

Domestic labor has always been a vital skill—worth learning and preserving. To understand this, we must embrace the stories that have been left out. BIPOC professionals have historically shaped how we build, clean, and organize our lives. When we make room for them, we foster a more inclusive and equitable vision of homemaking.

CHAPTER 16

THE SNOW WHITE EFFECT

THE INVITATION ARRIVED in my inbox: "KonMari x The Container Store VIP Mix and Mingle." There was a picture of Marie Kondo wearing a cream blouse, seraphically posed against a white backdrop. I accepted the invitation, curious to learn more.

A crowd of KonMari consultants, professional organizers, interior designers, and staff from the Container Store gathered around a table of donuts and boxed coffee. For most, it was a networking opportunity. For others, it was a chance to meet their idol. I parked myself near a professional organizer. Beside us, a KonMari consultant lurked and asked if any of us, too, had graduated from the KonMari program. We had not. She asked if we practiced the KonMari method. We did not. I shared an observation: "'Does it spark joy?' is a question we should ask ourselves, but it's not the only question."

"Exactly," the organizer beside me agreed. "A plunger doesn't spark joy, but we keep it around."

"But it does. My toilet brush sparks joy. It keeps my toilet clean, which makes me happy," the KonMari consultant replied.

It was then that Marie Kondo herself appeared. As she lightly skipped to the stage, she smiled and flirted with the audience, eyes batting slowly and brows rising gently. She once again wore a cream blouse, tucked neatly into a long navy skirt. She was thin and petite, with a delicate disposition. "You have to admit, she is cute," the organizer next to me whispered. As Kondo ministered her mission of tidying up the world, we delicately applauded.

She was at the Container Store to sell us her goods: tiny spice jars, bamboo hampers, and soft baskets made out of rope. After the pitch, Kondo's team invited each attendee to a photo op. Beyond having our cameras ready, we were to refrain from touching her. She stood like a wax figure while the women struggled to keep their hands to themselves. A group picture followed. Kondo raised her pointer finger—her signature pose that encapsulates the magic of tidying up. The women around her followed suit, smiling as they mimicked her gesture.

The Life-Changing Magic of Tidying Up was published in Japan when Kondo was in her mid-twenties. Her book became a global phenomenon, selling millions of copies and turning decluttering into an existential movement.[1] Later, she founded a worldwide certification program to train KonMari consultants who help people declutter by the KonMari method—which is to keep only things that spark joy.

Kondo, a self-proclaimed cleaning consultant, has enjoyed tidying up since she was five years old. She exemplifies the feminine ideal. She is a nonthreatening, cheerful, pretty, young figure who inspires us to embark on a delusional housekeeping quest for joy. Kondo's image—not her message—settles our trust. A cult of personality quiets questions because Kondo's persona aligns with an idea of femininity and homemaking with which we are well acquainted.

"Isn't it wonderful that tidying your house can enhance your beauty and contribute to a healthier, trimmer body?"[2] she writes. "It is as if your life has been touched by magic. Putting your house in order is the magic that creates a vibrant and happy life."[3]

Is it? In Kondo's practice, we thank our material possessions for their service. We thank our socks, coats, purses, and books. There is no emphasis on internal excavation or extension of personal gratitude, notwithstanding the spark of joy set off by our belongings. Her practice encourages us to eliminate what does not make us happy, all the while reinforcing that objects are where we find our happiness. This element of magic we are supposed to feel discounts the heavy load of housekeeping. When a woman like Kondo ignites a global movement, she channels deeply held ideals of gender, labor, and care.

* * *

THESE IDEALS found one of their earliest expressions in Walt Disney's *Snow White and the Seven Dwarfs*. The film premiered during the Great Depression as Disney's first feature-length animation, and Snow White was the original Disney princess. At the time, over 15 million people—predominantly men—were unemployed, leading to an influx of women entering the workforce.[4] Despite the nation's financial precarity, tensions rose as middle-class women went to work. Job scarcity for men had fractured the link between masculinity and financial gain.[5] A forecast of negative repercussions warned the nation that too many women entering the workforce would disrupt the delicate balance of gender roles in America. Fears spread that children with working mothers would go astray, jobs for men would remain scarce, and there would be no one to housekeep.[6]

"When you have more women working because of the Depression, you have a push towards not necessarily social equality but a sort of psychological equality,"[7] historian Carmenita Higginbotham explains. Higginbotham describes Snow White as "beautiful, aware of it, but not pushing for social change." It was a fantasy perfectly timed to recenter a society in flux.[8]

After fleeing the Evil Queen, Snow White stumbles upon a vacant cottage in the woods. Peering through the window, she spots an unkempt kitchen and several tiny beds. Judging by the mess, she assumes motherless children occupy the home. To her surprise, the filthy cottage belongs to seven grown men who, upon deliberation, let her stay in exchange for housekeeping.

"Now you wash the dishes. You tidy up the room. You clean the fireplace. And I'll use the broom." Cartoon chipmunks, deer, bunnies, and birds merrily follow Snow White's orders while she sings and dusts. Wild animals attempt unsanitary shortcuts, licking dishes clean and using their tails to sweep dirt under the rug. Snow White's gentle critique directs them as they stumble to the lake with dirty clothes for raccoons to scour on washboards and bluebirds to wring out to dry. By the end of the song, the entire cottage is spotless. Snow White, without a hair out of place, delivers on the promise of an immaculate turnaround if you whistle while you work.

As the prototype for Disney's princesses, Snow White was the ideal domestic. In fairy tales, housekeeping is an obstacle course made to determine the future of the young and pretty. Amid the chaos and villains, the heroine is polite, graceful, cheerful, and, above all, tidy. This formula would be repeated over and over. Princesses following the legacy of Snow White worked alongside fairy godmothers, animated brooms, and rodents to clean up messes that were never their own. They tidied up after masters, stepsisters, dwarfs, and wicked stepmothers. Their compliance was the gateway to their position as royalty.

The stark contrast between Snow White's isolation and the freedom of the Prince highlights the gendered burden of housekeeping. The Prince never had to sacrifice his happiness for domestic duties or live without servants. In contrast, heroines *were* the servants. They were also under immense societal pressure to marry well in order to escape a life of servitude. Without the Prince coming to her rescue, there'd be no happy ending.

Interestingly, most domestic icons embody Snow White's pleasing demeanor, reinforcing traditional femininity as inherently demure. Women who challenge or reject domestic ideals risk being cast as modern-day villains. Indeed, the Evil Queen became the prototype for Disney's early antagonists, a character who embodied the negative aspects of female power and agency. She was ambitious, opinionated, single, and mature. She owned her own property and was depicted as malicious, jealous, demanding, and conniving. These dysfunctional maternal figures oppressed potential princesses with chores to keep them from finding true love.

While fairy tales floated on dreams of magic, happy housekeeping, and romantic endings, the idea of effortless housekeeping has always been wishful thinking. At the time, domestic work was physically grueling. A homemaker had to master an assortment of tasks. Cooking and cleaning required exhaustive effort, consisting of arduous chores such as canning to preserve produce, polishing the silver, mending and sewing the clothes, dusting and mopping the floors. Before the ubiquity of washing machines, doing laundry required manually grinding the weight of wet clothes on washboards to rinse, wring, and repeat before hanging them out to dry.[9] Despite the labor a woman contributed to the space, the home was never wholly hers. The house belonged to the man—her father or husband—who could afford to pay for it. Gratitude and grace weren't only virtues, they were survival skills.

The pressure on women to perform went beyond completing their chores to smiling and looking good while doing them. In *The Art of Homemaking*, Daryl Hoole describes the ideal homemaker as a diamond. She should be "lovely to look at and lovely to be around—she has a wholesome attitude and a pleasing appearance. She has the courage to be happy and strives to live above the grievous faults of moodiness, sulkiness, and complaining."[10] Implicit in this message is the presence of a watchful eye. A woman's domestic labor, disposition, and personal presentation, even in the privacy of her home, was judged.

Good housekeeping etiquette omits a discussion of the frustrating and challenging aspects of homemaking. The normal, feminine woman would be happy staying home. One who was unhappy was, by definition, not normal. To reject the joy or transformation that housekeeping supposedly evoked was to be labeled unfeminine.[11] A homemaker who expressed unhappiness was considered as dangerous to society as a career woman was. In theory, both harbored a longing to distance themselves from the home.

Domestic labor presented to society as conceptually feminine is a manipulative tactic. Society uniformly assumes that if a woman has not mastered the art of domesticity, she has not mastered herself. The expectation for women is to nurture others, primarily through domestic labor, and to desire nothing more. Caring for the home was not merely a part of a woman's life. It was an all-consuming obligation that defined her identity.

Despite waves of feminist movements that brought women into the workplace, the division of domestic labor has not changed. Housework portrayed as merrily executed by women grooms viewers to believe they, too, must operate that way. This narrative instills an apprehension in women to redistribute any domestic responsibilities—out of fear of violating a feminine ideal. There is forever a battle in our minds between our human self, which can do only so much, and a social construct, which says we can do it all. I call this the "Snow White Effect." It's a societal expectation that creates a fantasy and masks a challenging reality. It's a myth that pressures women into performing the brunt of domestic labor without question, obscuring both the inequality embedded in these expectations and the personal toll it takes. In reality, domesticity consumes substantial time and energy. When it's unfairly distributed, it can block a woman's opportunities beyond the home.

This cultural narrative endured until the early 1960s, when voices like Betty Friedan's, in *The Feminine Mystique*, exposed the consequences of the homemaker ideal. Friedan wrote for her contemporaries—college-educated, middle-class housewives pressured to live up to commercial housewifery. The book examined the capitalist frenzy driving the homemaker trope.[12] More important, it called attention to the unhappiness and insecurity that women battled at home, despite supposedly fulfilling the American Dream. Freidan argued that women with non-domestic desires and dissatisfaction were not alone. This awakening paved the way for consciousness-raising groups and the modern feminist movement, revealing that there was more to life than homemaking.

I first read *The Feminine Mystique* during my senior year of high school. I had started a social group called Women Rule the World. We met once a month to talk about our roles in society, books, boys, and our dreams for the future. I didn't have the language to call our meetings political—we simply had a lot to say. We could feel, even then, that the deck was stacked against us. That larger forces were shaping our choices and nudging us toward paths we hadn't picked.

At that age, what struck me most about *The Feminine Mystique* was its focus on the "wife-mother-homemaker," as if the trifecta were singular. That to go from housekeeper to homemaker, a woman must first be a bride.

* * *

IN 2021, the television series *Marriage or Mortgage*, set in Nashville, Tennessee, made its Netflix debut. A short-lived reality show, it pitted a wedding planner against a real estate agent.[13] The hosts showed couples some houses and wedding venues, asking how they'd spend their savings (usually around $30,000). Should they splurge on a fairy-tale wedding or make a down payment on their dream home? The idea of investing in a house seems like it would outweigh the temptation to spend all of a couple's savings on a single day. After all, they could have their wedding in their backyard. Yet, in the end, the majority of couples chose the wedding.

In the interviews, many young women referred to it as "*my* dream wedding" as they discussed an event that would drain their savings in a few hours. "I've had literally everything planned to a tee since I was a little kid," one woman says.

"Pretty young to be thinking of a wedding," her fiancé laughs.

"I feel like every girl is like that."

Most couples on *Marriage or Mortgage* chose the wedding before buying a house because it is the expected order of events: First comes the wedding, then come the house and kids.

We don't see Snow White's wedding in the 1930s, but by the 1950s, Disney's wedding scenes were classic fairy-tale endings, with marriage as the final step in getting the keys to the castle. This scripted sequence reflects a broader social pattern: marriage as the gateway to a woman's domestic identity. Marriage seemingly validates everything that follows: her castle, herself, her worth.

Where Disney's fairy tale ends, the home and garden industry begins. The Snow White Effect remains visceral, as influencers on social media perpetuate the homemaker trope. Cheerful housewives, contentedly packing lunches and tidying homes, persistently reinforce the sexist expectations, thereby maintaining the problematic image Friedan questioned years ago.

Today's tradwives (traditional housewives) mirror the housewife propaganda of the 1950s and 1960s.[14] They demonstrate the fundamentalist-adjacent ideals in pristine spaces. One woman posted a picture of herself on Instagram wearing her wedding dress in her walk-in pantry. She posed in front of countless shelves of decanted dried food (no groom in sight).[15] Through flashy highlight reels, young mothers dressed in their best perform chores effortlessly, merrily, and, most important, alone.

On homemaking shows, we see married couples demonstrate domestic labor reflecting traditional gender stereotypes. We watch grown-ups play house while manly men execute heavy labor and resourceful women exhibit domestic creativity.

Single people—those organizing a studio apartment or otherwise making a home for themselves—are often cast as students, not experts. The millions of independent homeowners are absent from this spotlight, further linking the idea of home to the nuclear family.[16] This exclusion reinforces the idea that marriage is the gateway to legitimacy and that homes count only when their occupants follow traditional paths.

The fantasy is that domestic life begins when someone picks you. That our worth, our home, our future, starts when we're chosen. From domestic magazines to Instagram, HGTV to Netflix, these outdated social constructs of domesticity persist. As a result, many of us delay making a home because we're waiting for the total package.

Putting the spotlight on independent homemakers can broaden the public perception of what a home exemplifies. Women need not be wives or mothers to buy houses, nor embrace their homes fully. Similarly, a man does not need a woman to make a home for himself. Likewise, a woman's femininity is not contingent on her homemaking skills, nor is a man's masculinity defined by brute labor. Men and children have as much responsibility to nurture their spaces as do women.

For too long, women have been instructed to approach housework with a song in their hearts and optimism in their minds. The promise of a better life in a tidy space is a fantasy that has pressured women since the concept of home was feminized. Had the feminine ideal not been portrayed by young women housekeeping for others—in the castle, cottage, or dream house—would women measure their self-worth against it?

The truth is that there is nothing magical about housework. We don't have to whistle while we do it. We can care for spaces that reflect who we are and what we feel—and we can *happily* share that responsibility with others. Over the years, the feminine model has changed—even Disney's princesses have received a revamp. What hasn't changed, though, is the quiet expectation that a woman will disappear into the home she maintains. The real challenge for women today isn't tidying up—it's setting the boundaries between where the home ends and where she begins.

CHAPTER 17

PERFECTLY, PERFECT

IN THE MID-1800s, there were fewer than twenty millionaires in America. By the end of the nineteenth century, there were forty thousand. This period of staggering wealth became known as the Gilded Age—an era of economic growth and an emphasis on earthly treasures. A portion of this abundance was a result of the Industrial Revolution. Income taxes wouldn't be introduced until 1914, so privileged Americans gained inexhaustible resources without having to contribute to the public good.

The era's burgeoning industrialists and financiers understood that real estate was the hallmark of one's class. Their grand estates might boast a hundred or more rooms. Opening the doors for dinner parties, balls, and extended visits turned the most intimate settings into places to perform.

In *At Home: A Short Story of Private Life*, Bill Bryson notes that having servants to anticipate your needs was integral to the upper-class identity. The mansions and lifestyles these people upheld were so elaborate that some of their servants needed servants to meet all the demands.

Impeccability, Bryson argues, "generally only occurs to people who don't have to do the work themselves."[1] If the owner wanted the house redecorated overnight, the servants did it. If the owner wanted to throw a party and have their guests scavenge for jewels covered in sand, the servants arranged it and then cleaned up the mess. After every move the owner made—setting down a cup of tea, getting dressed, studying with books and papers scattered about the floor—rooms were restored to order as if by magic.

Popular preference then was to avoid seeing the help, so houses were constructed to prevent run-ins with them.[2] Many spaces designated for housework—like still rooms, pantries, storerooms, or some kitchens—were reached via pathways reserved for the workers. Dumbwaiters and service elevators maintained the distance between the effortless experiences of the wealthy and the grueling labor of the poor.

When slavery was abolished and income taxes were instituted, owning a mansion became less of a haven and more of a burden. The maintenance of these single-family houses became more challenging to afford. As population increases compressed the cities, developers pressured local governments to demolish the mansions occupying prime real estate on the city's main streets.[3] Vacant manors were torn down or renovated into multifamily units, apartments, and condominiums.

As modern inventions took on the nuances of housekeeping and servantry, more modest displays of wealth emerged in suburbia. The culture of mansions shifted to white picket fences, where domestic labor was no longer done by servants but, rather, by wives.

* * *

WHEN I WAS WORKING as a private cook, I used to dream of being the next Martha Stewart. I even cut her face out of a Macy's ad and pasted my own on top—her blond hair still intact, her white hands resting on a table decked out for the Fourth of July. I pinned the photo to my office corkboard and it hung there for years, part joke and part reverence for one of America's most extraordinary businesswomen.

Martha wasn't born into wealth. She grew up in a working-class family of eight. Her love for gardening wasn't a hobby—it was a necessity. Her mother was a teacher, and her father was a salesman who struggled to make ends meet. Consequently, her family had to grow their own food to eat and barter for what they couldn't produce.[4] Martha worked her way to the top. She started on Wall Street, which thrusted her into elite circles. Then she moved into catering for the wealthy. Her domestic creativity, her connections, and her fortitude led to book deals, TV shows, and a public company—making her the first female self-made billionaire in America.

Martha wasn't selling herself as the perfect woman. She didn't build her brand on being likable. She wasn't cute or innately playful. We didn't look to Martha for warmth. We looked to her for knowledge. She taught us how to tablescape, how to encase a turkey in puff pastry, how to stain floors, and how to make a holiday centerpiece. She sold us the fantasy of upward mobility through domestic mastery. She showed us how to access a lifestyle that was historically associated with wealth. That was the power of her brand.

Martha is proof that a girl from a working-class background can rise to the highest level of society—by renovating a house with her bare hands and hosting dinner parties that were the talk of the town. Martha wasn't *just* a homemaker. She didn't *just* cook, craft, and garden. She was an instructor who insisted we could create a lavish lifestyle for ourselves. She was saying, "This is how you do it. It's difficult but rewarding. Don't mess it up."

Women spent years comparing themselves to Martha. They took her business personally, believing that to be a good homemaker, they had to do it like she did it. But they weren't Martha. They didn't have teams of employees keeping their homemaking endeavors alive. Instead of their seeing her as a businesswoman, they looked at her as a measuring stick. No matter how many towels, containers, casserole dishes, and platters women bought, how many wreaths they learned how to make, or fitted sheets they learned to fold, they could never measure up.

Lifestyle branding convinces us that transformation is within our reach—if we try harder. The reality is that excellence isn't a one-woman show. Martha sourced her labor, had connections, and worked with the best of the best—the cream of the crop. None of these were sold to her consumers at Kmart.

When Martha faced adversity, the tabloids told us that she was "not so perfect" and was the "Queen of Mean." Yet the media weren't judging her by the standards of a CEO. They were judging her by housewife standards. If Marie Kondo exemplifies the Snow White Effect, then Martha Stewart personifies the Evil Queen. She built an empire, but the public didn't want an ambitious female entrepreneur. They wanted her to fit the homemaker mold. When she fell short of that impossible persona, her business suffered. In reality, Martha wasn't a woman who failed at homemaking. She was a woman who succeeded at business.

Martha's influence is everywhere—in the way we decorate, in the way we celebrate, in the way we buy into the idea of perfection as a product. She is the foundation for DIY and mainstream partnerships that have made the home and garden industry a cash cow. Her brand was never fully restored to the *Martha Stewart Living* we once knew. Although she's remained relevant over the years, she has become more of a personality than an educator. As a new wave of modern homemakers branded as sweet, fun, or wholesome has replaced her, perfection is still the product—yet none of them teach it like Martha.

In her absence, a new kind of authority has emerged: the professional home organizer. Unlike the Martha Stewart era, which centered on craftsmanship and on empowerment through knowledge, homemaking is now centered on styling—and what to buy to emulate the appearance of wealth.

* * *

"I AM SO PROUD of Khloe because this is something she did on her own. She paid for everything herself. She organized everything herself. She chose everything herself," Kris Jenner beams on an episode of *The Kardashians*, while Khloe shows off her organized pantry, closet, and home. "I got rid of a garage for this pantry," Khloe remarks as they admire the space. The camera pans across rows of white labels on clear jars and baskets stocked with enough dried goods to feed a village.[5]

My friend Becky and I chatted on the phone while reviewing photos of this pantry. Becky said, "Some people were like, 'Oh my gosh, this is amazing. I want my pantry to look like this.' Others were like, 'People are dying, we're in a pandemic, and you're showing off your pantry. Read the room!' I mean, who has a pantry that big?"

As I listened, I pulled up the post, zooming in and inspecting one shelf at a time.

"It's like a grocery store. You have to buy the same stuff to keep it looking like that. If you try anything new, it would throw it all off. Look at the cookies. Did you see the cookies stacked like a pyramid? I'd be afraid to eat them, I wouldn't want to mess them up."

I thought of organizers getting paid hundreds of dollars an hour to stack Oreos one cookie at a time. I thought of housekeepers earning a fraction of the cost to maintain them.

"I do like the jars with the labels on them," Becky continued. "I bought jars for my kitchen and got a chalk pen to write with. I know it's a pain in the butt to refill and relabel, but I have my granola, hemp seeds, and nuts in their own jars, and I've labeled each jar to say 'granola,' 'hemp seeds,' or 'nuts.'"

"Becky, you are the one who fills the jars. You can see through the glass. Why do you need labels?"

"Whenever I look at them, it makes me happy."

As a professional organizer, I understand the helpfulness of labels in certain situations. Labeling reminds us of the date we canned the tomatoes or the difference between cubed beef or goat in the freezer. It helps us orient young children to where things belong as they learn to put possessions away. Labeling can help us identify what is stored in drawer number three, which can save a lot of time when it's a chest full of drawers. However, labeling for decoration on decanted jars or baskets—to declare the obvious, "snacks," "pasta," or "paper towels"—goes beyond an aesthetically pleasing place marker and into a class marker.

Whether the person is designing the system or following one, labeling is rarely for ourselves and almost always for others. Sometimes, labels help us navigate what's been organized by someone else. For instance, organizers might label to assist disengaged house members in locating the contents in their space.

For those with staff, labeling acts as a road map for housekeepers, nannies, private chefs, house managers, and personal assistants to maintain things the way the home owner expects. For those without staff, who are actively engaged with their belongings, labeling isn't necessary. Women like Becky—who fill and empty, write and rewrite on the outsides of clear jars—like the way labels look. They also value what the labels represent—social distinction signaling not only what is inside but also that they can afford to maintain it.

"At the end of the day, these spaces we see on social media and on television are rarely made or maintained by the people who own them," I told Becky.

"Wait. You don't think it is possible to have a space this nice on your own?"

"No way. You have to have help. No one without help has the time to be doing all that. There's nothing wrong with having help, but let's not pretend it doesn't exist."

"But, I know plenty of women who have beautiful homes and work full-time, and they don't have help."

"They don't have any help?" I asked.

"No. They do it all themselves," she assured me.

"They don't have a house cleaner?"

"Well, yeah. They have a housekeeper who comes once a week."

"Becky, that's *help*."

Reality TV shows thrive on portraying superabundance. To situate the viewer, flashy montages of Rodeo Drive, sports cars, mansions, and organized closets set the stage for characters to flaunt their riches. What used to be kept behind closet doors has now entered the zeitgeist, and the presentation sells the lifestyle.

The visual of the successful man getting dressed in a walk-in closet, where nothing is out of place, is a classist trope. His cuff links are displayed neatly in compartments. His suits and ties are sorted by color. We admire his attention to detail. Glass shelves half-full of perfectly folded sweaters and rows of polished shoes validate his superiority. Without hearing a word, viewers understand that he can *afford* perfection.

When it comes to home organizing, influencers and organizing enthusiasts show off their cabinets, pantries, and closets on social media to highlight basic things that are set up in extraordinary ways. They elevate dried foods to an altar-like setting, precisely spacing and displaying them in pricey containers for the world to see. The elevation of necessities styled this way says, "We may own the same things, but the cost of caring for mine is astronomically higher."

It's not the items or systems that impress the audience, though. It's knowing what it takes to maintain them. Disposable income, time, and resources lend luxury to a picturesque home. Only in households with full-time hired help can things be constantly reset to an untouched neatness.

The media predominately portrays upper-class lifestyles as representing the "good life," keeping us wanting more. This is a resourceful business strategy aimed at consumers, but it's an exhausting way to live—constantly craving, wishing, overreaching, and pushing for a perfect outcome.

Behind every "Khloe organized this herself" shot, every social media post of a neatly dressed woman placing the final jar on the shelf, there's a hidden message: It's that perfection is possible with enough discipline, detachment, and bins.

Consequently, the illusion conceals the invisible labor, the support systems, and, for some, the privilege. The domestic presentation of control and effortless order isn't merely a display of tidy spaces. It's also a performance that subtly insinuates: "I'm perfect—because my home is perfect."

Social psychologist Thomas Curran, author of *The Perfection Trap*, suggests that perfectionism is rooted in a sense of lack and deficit that creates insecurity and feeds high standards.[6] These insecurities are expertly exploited by the home-organizing industry through performative perfection. This presentation isn't merely preference. It's shaped by a larger cultural narrative. The drive for flawless homes fuels overconsumption, waste, conspicuous spending, and insidious marketing to convince us that organization and the happiness it promises is something we must buy.

I have fallen prey to it, posting pictures of neat spaces on Instagram without acknowledging the work it took to create them. For years, I struggled to appreciate spaces that didn't meet my idea of perfection. When I had my *Jeffersons* moment and was moving on up to a fancier apartment, I believed I was fulfilling a dream. In reality, I was measuring my self-worth against material possessions and how I performed domesticity.

Looking back, it wasn't the new apartment that bothered me. It was the illusion that I would matter more once I moved into it. That the space—or my things—were proof I belonged to a superior class. I eventually realized that our sense of belonging isn't something we should buy. For so long, I thought upward mobility meant arrival, that if I curated a perfect home, I would finally feel worthy. The truth is, I was always worthy. In every version of every home, I mattered.

There was nothing wrong with the spaces I photographed and posted, but I framed them as if there were only one lifestyle deserving of attention. I had unconsciously internalized the very systems I sought to critique, valuing appearances over diversity. In short, the overemphasis on aesthetics shapes how we engage with the idea of home organization itself.

* * *

WHEN SOMEONE HIRES a professional organizer, the impetus is usually to make the space more functional and comfortable for themselves and others in the household. Something that often goes unspoken between the client and organizers is the expectation of an *organized aesthetic*, an accoutrement of labeled baskets and bins to contain their things.

At the start of the process, organizers help the client edit their belongings to make space for new systems. Once the decluttering is completed, the client often leaves while the organizers get to work. If we imagine what's shown on television, we see vans pull up with products—*lots* of products—and a team of women descends. Within hours, a miracle has occurred: Everything has a place, it's labeled, it's symmetrical, there is space to spare. The big reveal is emotional, as the client and organizers share tears and hugs. Then, the organizers wave goodbye while viewers get one final glimpse of what it's *supposed* to look like when we're organized. This is when the actual work begins.

It's one thing to attain an aspiration. It's another to maintain it. After the organizer leaves, the client must negotiate the ideal home within the realities of daily life. Some hire professional organizers to return monthly or seasonally, maintaining systems and managing the influx of stuff. Still, this upkeep comes at a cost of roughly $295 per hour for two organizers.[7]

If that cost can't be met, if organizers aren't rehired, the infrastructure becomes vulnerable to collapse. Three things threaten it: (1) limited resources to maintain the systems or the aesthetic established by the organizers, (2) overconsumption that outpaces the structure, and (3) a disengagement from the daily work of upkeep. Once perfection fades, disappointment tends to follow.

What we think of as organizing, which is often seen as the outcome—how neat your sock drawer is, how evenly spaced your glasses are, or how uniformly the baskets are sitting on an open shelf—are merely embellishments. They are the styling, the finishing touches to the systems themselves. The real work is the everyday work. Sustainability is essential to organizing.

We often forget to factor in the residual costs of what we buy into—the time, labor, and financial commitment required to maintain domestic perfection. We rarely ask ourselves whether the payoff is worth the price. At its core, organizing is about gathering information to create unique systems that work for *our* life. For that work to be effective, it has to be able to support us over time.

* * *

A CLIENT ONCE pointed out to me that the word *organize* derives from the word *organum* in Latin, or *organon* in Greek, meaning "instrument" or "tools." It shares its root with words like *organ*, the complex instrument that involves pedals, pipes, and keys that work together to make rich music. Or, consider organs like your kidneys, lungs, and heart, each with its particular function yet part of the whole body. Home organizing is a part of domestic labor. It's a form of housekeeping. This means that for the systems to work, they have to align with how we care for our spaces.

When we consume more than we can care for, or we create systems beyond what we can manage, we are overcompensating, trying to achieve an unattainable or unmaintainable lifestyle. We are complicating our lives at home so as to conform to an ideal that was created at a point in history when the responsibility of upkeep matched abundant labor.

CONCLUSION

THE POLITICS OF HOMEMAKING

IN 1983, a small group of women gathered in Los Angeles to explore the potential for offering a new service industry. The casual meeting became NAPO, the National Association of Professional Organizers, now known as the National Association of Productivity and Organizing Professionals. "What we learned very quickly was that the public, who were our potential clients, didn't understand what a professional organizer did," one founder reflected.[1] Organizing has always been a part of homemaking and housekeeping—spatial planning, decluttering, creating systems, project management, and coaching—but recognition as a standalone service was something new. This industry would grow to encompass home and office organizing, time management and productivity coaching, move management, and estate clearing.

It's worth noting that no formal education is required to become a professional organizer. Nevertheless, in pursuit of legitimacy, early organizers deliberately distanced themselves from homemakers and house cleaners, thereby reinforcing the class divisions within domestic labor. This strategic move was designed to command higher pay and more respect.[2]

To this day, some home organizers connect their work to that of therapists, in order to distance themselves from housekeepers. The act of separating themselves from the oppressive histories of domesticity has somehow allowed them to elevate one aspect of housekeeping while marginalizing another.

As I reflect on the complexities of homemaking, I am reminded of Tema Okun's work on white supremacy culture.[3] Okun describes how characteristics like perfectionism, sense of urgency, only one right way, and individualism are not merely personal habits but also pervasive cultural norms that affect how we navigate our lives and spaces.[4]

According to Okun, you don't have to be white to practice white supremacy culture thinking. These characteristics are not inherent to white people. Instead, they stem from a specific lifestyle, a "middle-class to upper-class, *wealthy* class whiteness."[5] In practice, white supremacy culture thinking disproportionately burdens BIPOC and working-class white people.

Okun's work emerged around the same time that NAPO took off and psychologists began studying perfectionism. The timing was not coincidental. They were all responding to societal demands for efficiency, control, and ideal homes and workplaces. Whereas organizers sought to harness these traits, psychologists and Okun challenged them, exposing how they perpetuate anxiety, burnout, and inequity.

* * *

THROUGHOUT THIS BOOK, I've explored the Soul Work that homemaking invites. Asking reflective questions allows us to let go in order to free our homes, hearts, and minds. This internal housekeeping lets us honestly assess why we hold on to possessions that no longer serve us as we confront clutter and the patterns of thought that perpetuate it.

Authentic homemaking, as I have learned, requires slowing down. The process invites us to engage with our spaces mindfully and to learn through seasons of discomfort. Homemaking is about both rejecting the urgency to conform to societal ideals and embracing the mundane domestic labor that we all have to do.

When we holistically engage in homemaking, we dismantle systemic forces that require us to leave parts of ourselves behind, to pursue an ideal. Reclaiming our homes means reclaiming the narrative about what home should be. It's resisting the pressure to live beyond our means and embracing the courage to live truthfully within them. It's consciously choosing joy—not as a superficial pursuit attached to things but as a deep expression of connection, our values, and purpose.

We can begin this work today, with the spaces we have, creating homes that reflect who we truly are, not who we're told we ought to be. Domesticity is an evolving practice. When we learn how to hold space for the ups and downs of this process, we learn a valuable lesson: how to make peace with our past and present.

When I launched Organize With Faith in 2014, I had no idea such profound lessons awaited me. Each client who graciously opened their home to me, every story they shared, and every victory and setback I witnessed contributed to a personal and professional transformation. Helping people achieve their goals has taught me a lot about life and how society influences our behavior, even within the sanctity of our homes.

For years, I didn't see my industry as part of the problem. I blamed injustice, patriarchy, racism, and income disparity. Yet these issues do lie at the heart of homemaking. The expectation that women should do the majority of domestic labor is a manifestation of the patriarchy. The predominance of white homemakers in the media reflects systemic racism. Invisible labor hides the fact that domestic perfection is never the work of a single individual and is sustained by the privilege of class. While these forces have historically shaped domestic life, we can change how we choose to engage with them.

We have the power to shape our environment. Every season of friction offers an opportunity to let the old way of doing things die and a new way to be born. Domestic labor isn't frivolous work. It's foundational work. When we recognize its influence, it becomes a conduit for change—a way to model how we care for ourselves and one another. In doing so, homemaking transcends the work of a single home and becomes a catalyst for public renewal.

In this light, homemaking is an intricate pattern of history and hope. It is how we record our stories. Each adjustment we make becomes a marker that maps our future. As we choose what stays and what goes, our sense of home takes shape. At its best, home becomes a testimony to all we have been through, and the love and acceptance we deserve.

SOUL WORK:

WORKBOOK

THE FIRST STEP toward getting organized is taken long before decluttering—it begins with you.

At Organize With Faith, we believe that faith isn't something you find at the finish line. It's the quiet confidence you carry every step of the way. We believe the homes we desire are possible, but more important, we believe that we are capable of making them.

This workbook is your space to tap into that belief for yourself. Through a series of reflective questions, you'll explore your past and your present so as to cultivate a more meaningful decluttering and organizing practice. You'll reconnect with your homemaking purpose and redefine your priorities with intention.

Keep this workbook close by you. Return to it when you need a reminder that transformation happens one step at a time. The journey to a home you love isn't by attaining perfection. It's achieved through faith, acceptance, and the courage to begin.

Let this be the start when you free yourself from the mental, emotional, and physical baggage that may be keeping you from creating a home that resonates with you.

I have included a few sample answers to get you started. Let's begin.

MIND AND MEMORY

1. What life transition has guided you to this book?

   EXAMPLE: Harry, my close friend and mentor, has passed, and I am now faced with the reality of life without him.

   ____

   ____

   ____

   ____

   ____

   ____

2. What are my top three goals for my home, and how do they align with the top three goals for myself?

   ____

   ____

   ____

   ____

   ____

   ____

3. What has shifted in your daily life, occupation, or social standing, and what changes have you made in your space to acknowledge that shift?

   EXAMPLE: I'm helping Harry's wife, Joanna, go through his belongings at home and in his office. As a result, I have an influx of his things in my apartment—things the family does not want and charities will not take. Harry's belongings have so much character and they remind me of what I love most about him. Since his personal items bear meaning for me, I will replace my things that are of no value and use his belongings instead. This replacement will allow me to integrate his possessions into my life.

4. What was your childhood home like, and in what ways does it differ or share similarities to your home now?

   EXAMPLE: As children, we deep-cleaned every Saturday. It was important to my mother that we kept the communal spaces clean. We could keep our bedrooms as clean or as messy as we liked. My room was never clean; I was messy. As an adult, I deep-clean my house and do my laundry every Saturday. I think the practice of tidying up as a child—but also the liberty of having a messy room—granted me permission to express myself the way

I wanted to in my space. Now my bedroom is clean, and I find myself tidying my room as a part of my chores. My home differs from my childhood home in that it is not closed off. My mother kept a private home. I host more than she did, and I have found I like a more open and hospitable space.

5. What home habits did you enjoy from your childhood, and what others would you like to change?

EXAMPLE: I love that I have adopted a spiritual relationship to my home. Growing up, I watched my mother pray and worship in our home, and I have worked on fostering that in mine. Something I did not like growing up was having the TV constantly on. Although I do not have a TV in my home now, I find myself spending too much time on the computer or my phone, which feels as distracting as the TV was in my childhood home. It takes me away from living a more meaningful life and cultivating more meaningful relationships.

6. What was the most difficult time in your life and how did you survive it?

   EXAMPLE: When I left my mother's home as a teenager, trying to figure out what was next for me—where I was going to live, or if my mother and I would ever heal our relationship—was extremely difficult. I survived because I focused on what was within my control. I made new friendships, I worked on creating the home and life I wanted for myself, I practiced boundaries with my mother, and I leaned on my support system.

FAITH

We do not have to be religious to have faith in something or someone. Ultimately, faith is our belief in things we cannot see or that are yet to come. In the context of home life, faith can serve as a guiding principle, influencing our daily routines, interactions, and the overall atmosphere of our living spaces. It provides a foundation for trust, hope, and resilience, enabling us to navigate challenges and celebrate joys within our homes. The following questions are meant to help you think about your faith and how it has influenced your life.

1. What do you have faith in, and what role does it play in your life?

____

____

____

____

____

____

____

2. My greatest strengths are:

____

____

____

____

____

____

____

3. My greatest challenges are:

PERSONALITY

1. I am quiet and reserved in my home when I . . .

   EXAMPLE: I am quiet and reserved in my home when I feel like I am on overload and need to decompress. When I have consumed too much information, or have gone through a difficult or stressful time, that is when I need silence to process things.

2. I am social and outgoing when I . . .

   EXAMPLE: When I am relaxed and I feel like all of my needs have been met.

3. I have changed over the last five years in the following ways. This is how I can see a reflection of those changes in my space.

4. What is my work-life balance and how does it make me feel?

5. I support myself in my space during stressful situations in these ways.

6. How is my definition of success reflected in my space?

   EXAMPLE: When I was younger I defined success by wealth—by the social signifiers that showed I was financially doing well.

   As I've gotten older, my definition of success has shifted. Now, it's defined by my relationships with the people I respect and love—their photos fill my space. Success to me, is also the quality of my free time, which I now spend gardening at my apartment and cabin.

RELATIONSHIPS

1. This is how I respect myself. These are my practices:

2. This is how I respect others:

3. When I am feeling anxious, overwhelmed, or full of love, how does my space reflect each of those emotions?

EXAMPLE: When I am feeling anxious, I distract myself by cleaning up. My house is impeccable when I have anxiety—it helps me work out my stress. When I am overwhelmed, my home is messy. Whenever I am overwhelmed, I spread papers all over my office, or clothes for an event all over my bed, trying to figure out what to wear. Having stuff everywhere helps me process intangible ideas. When I am feeling loved either by myself or others, the lighting is soft and my home is all about care. I find myself wanting to bask in caring for myself, and because of that I spend more time pampering and resting.

____

____

____

____

____

____

____

____

____

____

____

____

____

____

BODY CARE, SLEEP, AND ROUTINES

1. My bedtime routine is the following:

2. My bedroom supports my sleep habits in these ways:

3. The following helps me relax or fall asleep:

4. My morning routine is the following:

5. Is there room for improvement in my morning routine? If so, how?

6. My environment supports my physical well-being in these ways:

7. List any physical activities that you enjoy doing in your environment. For example, can you dance in your home? Can you lie down or rest in your home? Are these activities accessible? If not, how do you create space to make them more accessible?

8. How does the state of my kitchen affect my desire to nourish myself?

9. Does my kitchen meet my current needs? What simple things could I do to improve my kitchen?

COMMUNICATIONS AND PERSONAL EXPRESSION

1. How does the state of my space affect my viewpoint in going home—my mood—my feelings toward my home?

2. How does my environment shape my relationships with others?

3. What thoughts or insecurities limit my growth or block me from expressing myself to my fullest ability?

4. What areas within myself would I like to see healing or growth in, and how do I create space in my environment to do so?

5. What am I most passionate about, and how do I express my passion? How does it translate to my home?

6. What am I most grateful for in my space, and how do I express my gratitude in the space?

   EXAMPLE: I am most grateful for cultivating a home that is a place of peace. When life is stressful, I have a place to come home to that restores me. I am grateful for the quietness. I express my gratitude by being kind to my neighbors and putting things away toward the end of the day so I can get a head start in the morning without friction.

HOME

1. In what ways does my home serve me, and in what ways does my home restrict me?

2. Is getting organized important to me?

3. What domestic steps can I take to help me achieve my goals?

4. Do I share responsibilities around the house? If so, what do they look like? If not, what would I want them to look like?

5. What home patterns have migrated with me as I've moved to new locations?

6. This is how I care for my space:

   EXAMPLE: I clean up after myself. I keep my refrigerator well stocked, and I buy only what I can eat so I do not waste food. I get things fixed when they are broken. I keep a list of things that need to be done so they are not forgotten. I water my plants. I get rid of things that are useless so my space does not become a graveyard of junk. I let go of whatever no longer serves me and the space.

7. This is how I ask others to care for my space:

8. Each room in my home is filled with . . .

EXAMPLE: Love, beauty, color, and things that remind me of my loved ones and my history.

9. My home reflects my . . .

EXAMPLE: My home reflects my hard work, creativity, and determination. I find that whatever I am working on, I am surrounded by it in my home. Whether it is the book I am writing or new projects, whatever is a priority in my life at the moment takes center stage in my environment. I prioritize the things that matter to me the most, and I allow them to take up space in my home.

10. These are colors that soothe me:

11. This is how I display objects that are meaningful to me:

12. In gathering this understanding, how has it affected me mentally, spiritually, and physically?

13. What patterns do you notice in your habits, values, and desires? How do your past homes reflect your inner life? How can these insights guide the home you're creating now?

14. I feel inspired to do ____________________ in my space. What three steps can I do to make it so?

GLOSSARY OF KEY ORGANIZING TERMS

Category/Categorizing: A collection of similar things that complement one another, forming a small part of a larger interconnected system.

Containers/Containing: The corralling of objects in one place or receptacle.

Maintenance: The regular care of your space and organized systems. Also known as a refresh—tidying, refolding, realigning, decluttering, and color-coding, so order is sustained.

Mindfulness: Letting go of rigid ideas of how things "should" be organized, and instead focusing on systems that support your needs and sensitivities, and how you actually live.

Minor Manipulations: Micro-adjustments, tweaks in placement to help make a system more user-friendly.

Modifications: Larger changes, the relocation of zones or categories to help improve the network.

Network: The intersection of all categories and zones, it is the overarching organization of a space, in its entirety.

Placement: The act of setting items or categories in a temporary or final location.

Reorganization: Corrections to part of a system when it's no longer working or not user-friendly.

Revisions: A full-scale redesign when systems or networks no longer serve the household.

Sorting: The pulling out of everything from a selected space and dividing it like with like.

Spatial Mapping: A visual floor plan that illustrates the location of categories and zones.

System: A set of placements that form a functional unit within a zone.

Zone/Zoning: The strategic areas in a network system. Zones are the assigned locations for either executing specific tasks, or storing a related group of items, directing the flow, and ensuring the efficiency of the network system.

ACKNOWLEDGMENTS

To Kara Watson, my editor—you are a blessing. Thank you for finding me. Thank you for hearing the voice I had buried and long abandoned, and for patiently teasing it out of me.

To my agents, Tanya McKinnon and Carol Taylor—Tanya, thank you for believing in this work from the start. Carol, thank you for answering the call (literally) at the eleventh hour. You helped me cross the finish line with my sanity intact. Your insight and guidance were instrumental.

To Azeen—thank you for helping me see the whole when I saw only fragments.

To the friends who've listened to me rant, laugh, spiral, and spiral again about my industry—you've fueled my suspicions, entertained my research, read my writing, and made it all more joyful. Thank you for your love and support.

To my brilliant baby cousin Kennis and to Kyle and Alessandra—thank you for combing through every last bit of HGTV data to confirm I wasn't crazy.

To my team at Organize With Faith, past and present—you've helped build and carry this business, often holding the torch while I ran off to write. Thank you for keeping the light on.

To my clients—thank you for sharing your homes and your stories with me. You've shaped this book more than you know.

To the mentors and champions who helped me hone both my message and my mission, Ms. Lassiter, Diana, Mr. Shaeffer, Kelsey, Latoya, Ronda, Mirko, Melanie, Meriamne, Mark, Peter, and Kartini—thank you.

To my brother, Kevin—thank you for that one dinner when you said, "You need reflective questions." You were absolutely right.

To my parents—complex, loving, funny, brilliant, and oh-so-human. You are the reason I do what I do the way I do it. You've given me the gifts of courage, curiosity, and faith. Thank you for challenging me, loving me, cheering me on, and making me fearless. Daddy, thank you for reading this manuscript out loud with me, over and over again.

To my partner—whom I met shortly after planting my love garden, who waters the flowers when I am away and helps me lug mulch from the nursery—I love you.

Above all, thank you to the Divine Spirit—for being a light and a constant, for guiding me toward people I can learn from and offer something to in return. Thank you for comforting me at my lowest and blessing me with these dreamy opportunities. Thank you for your grace.

To the beautiful community around me—thank you. I am held, heard, and wildly grateful.

NOTES

Chapter 15: Opportunity Denied

1. Emily J. Heller, "A Billion-Dollar Dream: How HGTV Took Over Cable," *Vanity Fair*, April 2021.
2. Richard Lawson, "Home Truths: How HGTV, Magnolia, and Netflix Are Building a Massive Space in the Stream," *Vanity Fair*, May 2021.
3. HGTV Network, "HGTV's Black History Month Commercial," February 2021.
4. Lawson, "Home Truths."
5. HGTV, "HGTV Airing Schedule, 2022," HGTV.com.
6. Anthony Szczesiul, *The Southern Hospitality Myth: Ethics, Politics, Race, and American Memory* (Athens: University of Georgia Press, 2017), 12.
7. Szczesiul, *The Southern Hospitality Myth*, 7.
8. *The Progressive Farmer* (Birmingham: Southern Progress Corporation, October 1963).
9. *4 Little Girls*, directed by Spike Lee (New York: HBO Documentary Films, 1997).
10. John Logue and Gary McCalla, *Life at Southern Living: A Sort of Memoir* (Baton Rouge: Louisiana State University Press, 2000), 31, 34.
11. Advertisement, Whirlpool, *Better Homes and Gardens* 43, no. 3 (March 1965).
12. Tara McPherson, *Reconstructing Dixie: Race, Gender, and Nostalgia in the Imagined South* (Durham, NC: Duke University Press, 2003), 7.
13. Enobong Hannah Branch, *Opportunity Denied: Limiting Black Women to Devaluing Work* (New Brunswick, NJ: Rutgers University Press, 2011), 49–70.
14. Esther Cooper Jackson, "The Negro Woman Domestic Worker in Relation to Trade Unionism," *Viewpoint Magazine*, 2015 [orig. 1940], https://

viewpointmag.com/2015/10/31/the-negro-woman-domestic-worker-in-relation-to-trade-unionism-1940/.

15. Makoroba Sow, "Help Wanted: The Bronx Slave Markets and the Exploitation of Black Women Domestic Workers," *NYPL Blog*, New York Public Library, April 15, 2022, https://www.nypl.org/blog/2022/04/15/bronx-slave-markets.
16. Rachael DeLaCruz, "Bracero Families: Mexican Women and Children in the United States, 1942–64" (MA thesis, Old Dominion University, 2015), DOI: 10.25777/d25j-ad84, https://digitalcommons.odu.edu/history_etds/112.
17. Yolanda Chávez Leyva, "'Faithful Hard-Working Mexican Hands': Mexicana Workers During the Great Depression," *Perspectives in Mexican American Studies* 5 (1995): 66–78, https://arizona.aws.openrepository.com/handle/10150/624819?show=full.
18. Larisa L. Veloz, *Even the Women Are Leaving: Migrants Making Mexican America, 1890–1965* (Oakland, CA: University of California Press), https://www.ucpress.edu/books/even-the-women-are-leaving/paper.
19. "TikTok's Queen of Clean Vanesa Amaro Shares Her Top Cleaning Hack for 2023." YouTube video, 2:37. Posted March 29, 2023. https://youtu.be/_ZhSqSlLzDg.

Chapter 16: The Snow White Effect

1. Emilia Petrarca, "The Queen of Decluttering Would Like to Sell You Some Things." *The Cut*, November 18, 2019, https://www.thecut.com/2019/11/marie-kondo-konmari-store.html.
2. Marie Kondo, *The Life-Changing Magic of Tidying Up* (New York: Ten Speed Press, 2014), 195.
3. Kondo, *The Life-Changing Magic of Tidying Up*, 127.
4. Jessica Pearce Rotondi, "Underpaid, But Employed: How the Great Depression Affected Working Women," History.com, March 11, 2019, updated August 19, 2025, https://www.history.com/articles/working-women-great-depression.
5. Jane Batkin, "Framing Snow White: Preservation, Nostalgia and the American Way in the 1930s," in *Snow White and the Seven Dwarfs: New Perspectives on Production, Reception, Legacy* (New York: Bloomsbury Academic, 2021) 151, 157, 158, https://repository.lincoln.ac.uk/articles

/chapter/Framing_Snow_White_Preservation_Nostalgia_and_the_American_Way_in_the_1930s/24391465.

6. Estelle B. Freedman, "The New Woman: Changing Views of Women in the 1920s," *The Journal of American History* 61, no. 2 (September 1974): 378–82, https://www.jstor.org/stable/1903954.
7. Carmenita Higginbotham, "Snow White: The Ideal 1930s Woman," *American Experience*, PBS, https://www.pbs.org/wgbh/americanexperience/features/snow-white-ideal-1930s-woman/.
8. Batkin, "Framing Snow White."
9. Glenna Matthews, "*Just a Housewife*": *The Rise and Fall of Domesticity in America* (New York: Oxford University Press, 2004), 98–99.
10. Daryl Hoole, *The Art of Homemaking* (New York: Harper & Row, 1963), 2–5.
11. Glenna Matthews, "*Just a Housewife*," 211.
12. Betty Friedan, *The Feminine Mystique* (New York: W. W. Norton, 1963), 15, 18, 20, 32, 50–51.
13. *Marriage or Mortgage*, season 1, episode 9, "Out of the Friendzone," aired March 10, 2021, on Netflix.
14. Joy Reid, "Katie Britt's Mocked GOP Rebuttal Part of Conservatives' 'Trad Wives' Plan to Send Women Back to the Kitchen," *The ReidOut*, MSNBC, https://www.msnbc.com/the-reidout/watch/katie-britt-s-mocked-gop-rebuttal-part-of-conservatives-trad-wives-plan-to-send-women-back-to-the-kitchen-206211141515.
15. Alice Murphy, "Bride, 28, Defends Herself Against Cruel Trolls' 'Disgusting' Comments After Sharing Wedding Photos of Her Posing Inside Her Organised Pantry," *Daily Mail*, April 8, 2021, https://www.dailymail.co.uk/lifestyle/article-9451781/Australian-bride-defends-trolled-taking-wedding-photos-pantry.html.
16. Michael Kolomatsky, "Single Women Own More Homes Than Single Men," *The New York Times*, February 2, 2023, https://www.nytimes.com/2023/02/02/realestate/single-women-own-more-homes-than-single-men.html.

Chapter 17: Perfectly, Perfect

1. Bill Bryson, *At Home: A Short History of Private Life* (New York: Vintage, 2011), 98, 102, 234–35, 251.
2. Bryson, *At Home*.

3. Brian Coffey, "The Changing Form and Function of Urban Mansion Districts: The Example of Rochester, New York," *International Society for Landscape, Place & Material Culture* vol. 23, no. 1 (1991): 15–22, https://www.jstor.org/stable/29763865.
4. R. J. Cutler, dir. *Martha.* Netflix, 2024, https://www.netflix.com/title/81479059.
5. *The Kardashians*, season 1, episode 7, "Where I've Been and Where I Wanna Go," aired May 26, 2022, on Hulu.
6. Dan Harris, host, *10% Happier with Dan Harris*, podcast, episode 767, "The Science Of Overcoming Perfectionism | Thomas Curran," May 6, 2024, https://www.tenpercent.com/tph/podcast-episode/thomas-curran.
7. "The Gurus of Tidiness: If You Like Marie Kondo . . . ," *The New York Times*, March 27, 2019, https://www.nytimes.com/2019/03/27/style/marie-kondo-cleaning-gurus.html.

Conclusion: The Politics of Homemaking

1. "NAPO 30th Anniversary—Founders," posted April 30, 2015, by NAPO, YouTube, https://www.youtube.com/watch?v=egTU_C5BkYw.
2. Carrie M. Lane, *More Than Pretty Boxes: How the Rise of Professional Organizing Shows Us the Way We Work Isn't Working* (University of Chicago Press, 2024), pp. 31–49.
3. Kenneth Jones and Tema Okun, "White Supremacy Culture, A Summary," In *Dismantling Racism: A Workbook for Social Change Groups* (Durham, NC: ChangeWork, 2001), https://mn.gov/olmstead/assets/White%20Supremacy%20Culture_tcm1143-487343.pdf.
4. The Intercept, *Deconstructed*, podcast, season 10, episode 5, "Tema Okun on Her Mythical Paper on White Supremacy," Febuary 3, 2023, https://shows.acast.com/deconstructed/episodes/tema-okun-on-her-mythical-paper-on-white-supremacy.
5. "Webinar: White Supremacy Culture—A Conversation with Tema Okun, PhD," Society for the Psychological Study of Social Issues (SPSSI), posted April 25, 2022, YouTube, https://www.youtube.com/watch?v=IzcLYONE_7Q.